MW01140736

ELIZABETH COELHO / MOIRA WONG

My Country, Our History

Canada from 1867 to the Present

Teacher's Resource Book

Burnaby South Secondary School
5455 Rumble St.
Burnaby BC
V5J 2B7

012043

Pippin Publishing

Copyright ©1996 by Pippin Publishing Corporation
Suite 232
85 Ellesmere Road
Toronto
Ontario M1R 4B9

All rights reserved. Reproducible pages may be photocopied for
classroom use only. Otherwise, no part of this publication may be
reproduced or transmitted in any form or by any means,
electronic, mechanical, or otherwise, including photocopying and
recording, or stored in a retrieval system without permission
in writing from the publisher.

Designed by John Zehethofer
Edited by Dyanne Rivers
Typeset by Jay Tee Graphics Ltd.
Printed and bound in Canada by Brown Book Company Limited

Canadian Cataloguing in Publication Data

Coelho, Elizabeth, 1946-
    My country, our history : Canada from 1867 to the present.
        Teacher's resource book

Supplement to: Hux, Allan D., 1948-   . My country, our
history : Canada from 1867 to the present.
ISBN 0-88751-059-0

1. Reading (Adult education).   2. Reading — Remedial teaching.
3. Language arts — Remedial teaching.   4. English language —
study and teaching as a second language.   5. Canada — History
— Study and teaching.   I. Wong, Moira.   II. Hux, Allan D.,
1948-   My country, our history: Canada from 1867 to the
present.   III. Title.

FC170.H922 1995   428.6′2   C95-932109-8
F1026.H922 1995

ISBN 0-88751-059-0

10 9 8 7 6 5 4 3 2

Contents

Introduction

This resource guide is designed to accompany *My Country, Our History*, which is an introduction to Canadian history for middle and secondary school students, as well as students in adult education programs.

My Country, Our History

The student's book was written especially for classes in which some or all of the learners are recent arrivals in Canada or are returning to school as adults. Existing textbooks are often inappropriate for these learners because:

- They assume that the learners have been exposed to a great deal of information about Canada and are familiar with important themes and concepts such as Canada's First Nations, imperialism and colonialism, European conquest and settlement, the annihilation or displacement of First Nations groups, Confederation, French-English relations, relations between Canada and the United States, land rights and multiculturalism. This knowledge is essential not only as important background the studying of Canadian history, but also as cultural and political background for students who are coming to Canada to live and participate as informed citizens. We can't assume that students who have not been involved in the Canadian education system through elementary and middle school have this knowledge.
- They assume that all students are familiar with the teaching and learning styles prevalent in North American schools.
- They assume a level of proficiency in English that most recent arrivals will take at least five years to acquire, and that many returning adults do not have.

My Country, Our History assumes that students have little or no previous knowledge of Canada. Themes in Canadian history are presented sequentially, using a chronological approach and drawing parallels with students' knowledge of similar concepts in different contexts. The language used in the text is also presented in sequence; the opening chapters are short and simply written. As students work through the text, however, the chapters become a little longer and more complex sentence patterns are introduced and reinforced. Pre-reading questions are provided to guide the reader and important vocabulary is highlighted in the text. New words and sentence patterns are recycled in subsequent chapters.

My Country, Our History: Teacher's Resource Book

The resource book is designed to integrate the study of history with the development of language skills, particularly the skills required for academic study. The activities are designed to help students understand the text, participate in classroom activities, and refine their English-language skills at the same time.

The resource book is arranged in three sections:

- The first explains how to use the textbook, guiding the students' reading and helping them develop effective reading skills for academic study.
- The second consists of teaching notes for each chapter of the textbook. These notes identify some key features of the text, explain how to use the activity pages in conjunction with the content of the chapter, and suggest extension activities.

• The third consists of reproducible pages containing student activities for use with each chapter. These activities are designed to integrate language and content through the use of graphic organizers, cloze activities, vocabulary puzzles, group activities, structured writing tasks and independent writing assignments, and simulation and roleplay. These pages can be duplicated for classroom use.

How to Use the Textbook

Many students find academic text difficult to read. They may, for example, try to process text word by word, stopping whenever they encounter unfamiliar vocabulary. This is an inefficient approach that slows the reading and hinders comprehension of the main ideas and the relationships among ideas in the text.

Reading expository text involves the skilful use of several related strategies. Most students need support to develop these skills. Teachers can provide this support by intervening between students and text to guide the reading process. This approach helps students gain information from texts that are beyond their independent reading level and develop reading strategies that enable them to become more independent readers of difficult material. The process can be modified to help students obtain information from videos and other audiovisual materials.

The activities suggested in this resource book are based on a three-part approach to guided reading: pre-reading, reading and post-reading. To use *My Country, Our History* most effectively, it's a good idea to include each of these stages when planning lessons.

Pre-Reading

The following are some strategies that help prepare the students for the material they are going to read:

Group Brainstorming

Brainstorming is a wonderful way to generate ideas. Although brainstorming sessions are often conducted with the whole class, group brainstorming provides more support for many students, especially those who are new to Canada and may not have experienced this kind of activity before or those who may be intimidated at the prospect of speaking English in front of the entire class.

Brainstorming can be used before or after reading to encourage students to speculate about alternatives (what if...?). Brainstorming is also useful for problem-solving and generating ideas for projects.

This is how the process works:

• Assign the discussion task and lay the ground rules: all ideas are welcome; no idea is too crazy at this stage; everyone has the right to pass; etc.
• Establish a time limit.
• Record the ideas that have been generated, being sure to acknowledge each group's work. For example, take one idea at a time from each group until all the ideas are listed on the chalkboard or chart. Another time, encourage the groups to send representatives to look at the work of other groups and bring back useful ideas, or double up the groups so they can present their ideas to each other.
• Another approach is the "gallery walk." Each group creates a chart, list or mind map categorizing their ideas and posts it on the classroom wall. Two members of the group stay with the chart to explain it to students from other groups while their partners walk around the room, looking at the charts developed by the other groups. Then, explainers and walkers switch roles.

When all the students have finished the walk, they return to their own groups and revise their visuals to include new ideas.

- Guide the students in a survey of the text. Direct their attention to helpful features such as the table of contents, the chapter title pages and chapter introductions, the questions that serve as subheadings, the highlighted words, the supplementary information in the margins, visual material such as maps, charts, graphs and photographs, and the questions at the end of each major section of text. Efficient readers use these aids to get a sense of the organization and content of a text and to enhance their comprehension.
- Use pictures, photographs, films, speakers, field trips, other concrete materials and literature to develop interest in and background knowledge of the passage to be read. The chapter title pages can help orient students to the content of the chapter.
- Relate what students already know about the topic to what may be new to them. For example, most ESL learners have a knowledge of government in other countries. It makes sense to activate this before introducing the material on government in Canada.
- Organize small-group brainstorming sessions to activate students' previous knowledge and stimulate interest. Encourage them to look at the chapter title page and predict the content of the chapter or write several key words from the passage or chapter on the board and invite them to predict how these words might be related to the material they are going to read.

- A KWL chart (what we know, what we want to learn, what we learned) often helps students organize their thinking. Before reading, invite them to complete the first two sections. Once they are finished reading, revise and complete the chart. Using this strategy is especially helpful before starting a major unit of study, such as Canada and World War I, and in preparing for independent study projects.

Know	Want to Learn	Learned

- Establish a purpose for reading by asking students to, for example, find out how Canada became a nation. In *My Country, Our History*, the purpose is stated at the beginning of each chapter and each section; however, because some students are so anxious to get on with the task of reading the text, they may miss helpful aids of this kind. As a result, it is important to direct their attention to the chapter introduction and guiding questions.
- Provide a graphic organizer to show students how the chapter is organized and how the main ideas are related. Graphic organizers are visual representations of the content, showing how the information and

How to Use Graphic Organizers

Graphic organizers can be used in a variety of ways:

- Show students a blank or partially completed organizer to preview the organization of a section of text or the information in the text.
- Give students an organizer to complete during a reading or viewing. This will help them read or view with a purpose.
- Use an organizer to help generate language patterns that express how ideas are related; for example, to relate cause and effect or show a chronological sequence.
- Use an organizer as an evaluation tool. As part of a test or assignment, students can complete a blank or partially completed organizer that they have already used in class.
- Encourage students to use organizers as a pre-writing strategy to help organize their ideas or as a study aid when preparing for tests or exams.

ideas in a textbook, unit or lesson are organized. Examples include timelines, charts, graphs, flow charts, Venn diagrams, classification trees and concept maps. Representing a concept or main idea visually reduces the linguistic demands on the students and enables them to "see" the relationships among ideas.

The reproducible activity pages in this resource book include at least one graphic organizer for each chapter, providing an overview of the content of the chapter and representing relationships such as generalization and example, cause and effect, comparison and sequence.

- Pre-teach a few key words. These should be words that will greatly enhance the students' comprehension of the text. In *My Country, Our History*, key words that may be new to some students are highlighted in the text. Do not, however, pre-teach *all* new vocabulary; students need to develop their own strategies for dealing with the new words they encounter in a text. Some of these strategies are outlined in the following section.

Reading

Efficient readers read textbooks and other expository material in different ways, according to their purpose. For example, they may skim to get a general idea, then return to read specific sections in more detail.

Developing readers need the direction and support provided by guided reading to develop these strategic reading skills. Use some of the following strategies to provide this direction and support:

- Direct students to read chunks of text silently—or follow the text while you read aloud—with a specific question or purpose in mind. For example, you may ask them to identify the main idea of a passage or locate the topic sentence in a paragraph. In *My Country, Our History*, guiding questions are provided before each section of text and discussion questions are included at the end of each section.

- "Jigsaw" some of the text so that each student in a group is responsible for a specific section of the chapter. For an example of how to do this, see the lesson notes and activity pages for Chapter 6.

- Provide questions that refer the students back to the text to find specific details that exemplify, support or clarify the main idea, concept or principle. In *My Country, Our History*, the paragraphs are numbered for ease of reference. Students might use the information to complete a graphic organizer or read aloud the phrase or sentence(s) that answers a specific question.

- Instruct students to find specific words in context and make inferences about the meanings of the words. *My Country, Our History* provides contextual support for new or difficult words; the paragraphs are numbered and words are highlighted so that students can find the words easily and refer to the context.

- Encourage students to use a dictionary only as a last resort. Teach them how to use monolingual learners' dictionaries. The best of these provide a pronunciation key, simple explanations, and examples in a clear context. Most students, including many who are fluent in English, will find these more helpful than large reference dictionaries that assume that the reader has a lot of experience with dictionaries, a large vocabulary and sophisticated knowledge of the parts of speech and usage labels. Your ESL department probably has a set of dictionaries that you can use.

- Direct the students' attention to the photographs, charts and other visual materials that support the text, and ask questions designed to show that these materials provide specific information. Sample activities using the visual material are included for Chapters 1, 5 and 7.

- Use the case studies, the material in Canadians Who Make a Difference and the sidebar material to enrich the text. The linguistic complexity of this material is not controlled in the same way as the main text; some of it is archival material and linguistically quite difficult. Rather than focusing on total comprehension for all students, help them "get the flavour" of the language and a general understanding of the content and how it relates to the main text. One strategy involves reading this material aloud to students while they follow in the text, then leading a brief discussion of the content.

Post-Reading Activities

At this stage, it's helpful to introduce activities that encourage students to review and reinforce what they have read, engage in group discussion or problem-solving related to the content of the chapter, and focus on specific items such as transition words, grammar patterns or new vocabulary. Many of the reproducible activity pages in this resource book are designed to be used at this stage of the reading process.

• Discuss what students now know about the topic, story or passage. Students can summarize and review the chapter by completing a graphic organizer. Focus on vocabulary. Encourage students to record new words in a special vocabulary notebook. In addition to copying the sentence(s) in which the word occurred, suggest that they include an explanation or translation if necessary. The following techniques are also helpful:
— Word puzzles help students both learn new words by relating them semantically to the content of a lesson and recognize specific patterns by directing their attention to surface features such as sound-symbol correspondence, affixes, etc. The activity pages in this resource book include several different kinds of puzzles.
— Word analysis is helpful for many Latin-based words. Help students develop their word analysis skills by studying stems and affixes and relating new vocabulary to antonyms, synonyms,

etc. The reproducible pages for the first few chapters include activities to help students develop their awareness of how words are related and their word-analysis skills.
— Cloze activities based on the content of a text or lesson provide opportunities for students to practise using specific features of language in a supported context while reviewing content. Cloze passages require students to supply key words that have been deleted from a passage of text that summarizes or paraphrases information from the text or lesson.

The cloze technique is equally useful as an evaluation tool. Many of the cloze passages in this resource guide can be used for both purposes.

The Cloze Technique

Traditional cloze passages, from which words are deleted in a specific pattern, are sometimes used as one measure of the readability of a text in an effort to match students with texts at their comprehension level. Targeted cloze passages, on the other hand, are a useful strategy for encouraging students to use language in context.

Targeted cloze passages delete specific kinds of words from the text:

• New vocabulary.
• The correct form of a word (noun, verb, adjective, etc.) in a "word family."
• A specific verb form, such as passive voice or verbs in the past perfect tense.
• Transition words and phrases that indicate how ideas are related. These may, for example, demonstrate sequence or cause and effect.

Some students may need a list of words or phrases to choose from; others may prefer to work without a list, checking their work against the list later.

About English Pronunciation Did You Know...?

- Because many English words do not follow common spelling and pronunciation conventions, students may have trouble when they first encounter them in print and try to "decode" them into speech. For example, students using common phonics rules may pronounce *Métis* as *Met-iz* or *Met-iss*, *Vancouver* as *Van-cow-ver*, *courage* as *cow-rage* and *imagine* as *im-a-jine*.
- Some students may need help with English sounds that do not exist in their home language. For example, the sounds represented by *th* in English, as in *these*, *although*, *therefore* and *math*, do not occur in most other languages.
- Stress is as important as producing vowel and consonant sounds. For example, it is important to distinguish between "He read his **story**" and "He read **his**tory."
- Words of two or more syllables, such as *colony*, *municipal*, *Confederation* and *Newfoundland*, may present difficulties for learners who don't know where the stress should fall.
- The stress in some words changes according to the way they are used. For example, *re-'cord* is a verb, but *'re cord* is a noun.
- The main stress in a word often changes when affixes are added (e.g., *democrat*, *democracy*, *democratic*).

- Highlight special function words such as "therefore," "as a result (of)," "because (of)," "although," etc. and explain how they help readers both understand how ideas are related and predict what is coming next. The reproducible activity pages in this resource book include structured writing activities that help students understand and use these words.
- Include pronunciation practice of new words so that students can recognize and use them orally as well as in print. Articulate carefully and invite students to repeat, chorally and individually. Lead students in choral readings of sentences and paragraphs to help them develop a feel for the rhythm and intonation patterns of English.
- Organize group activities designed to encourage students to return to the text. For example, ask each group to prepare written questions on a specific section of the chapter, then give the questions to other groups to answer, either orally or in writing.
- Show students how to paraphrase key sentences from the passage. The teaching notes for Chapters 3 and 8 provide examples of how to do this.
- Explain features of grammar that are important to or recur in the context of the study of history. In *My Country, Our History*, each chapter focuses on one or two grammatical features, such as the past perfect tense, passive verbs or the affix system. The reproducible activity pages in this resource book include grammar explanations followed by structured writing activities that encourage students to practise the linguistic feature(s) highlighted in the chapter.
- Provide literary experiences that support or extend the themes in the text: introduce poems, narrative, biographical or archival material. Examples and suggestions are included in both the teaching notes and reproducible activity pages.
- Assign independent writing tasks in a variety of formats — journal responses, letters, newspaper reports and editorials, graphs, charts and lists or tables, instructions and recipes, poems, scripts and stories, as well as exposition. The teaching notes in this resource book include suggestions for journals and other writing assignments. Students may select some of these pieces to develop through the writing process and submit them for evaluation.
- Provide writing "scaffolds" to guide and support the students' writing. For example, some students might need a "starter

sentence" to help them get started on a journal response.

For expository writing, a paragraph frame consisting of a topic sentence and a few link words can provide a scaffold for composition. Activities using writing scaffolds are included in the reproducible activity pages for every chapter.

- Involve students in roleplays, simulations and problem-solving activities based on the content of the lesson or textbook. Both the teaching notes and reproducible activity pages in this resource book include some of these activities.
- Provide experiences that will enrich and extend the classroom program: field trips, movies, classroom visitors, music and song, visual arts and cultural artifacts, dramatic performances, TV and radio news programs, and a variety of print media. The teaching notes and learning materials in this resource book include some of these activities.
- Include some guided research projects, starting with very simple information-gathering tasks, to introduce students to this way of learning. Provide plenty of in-class guidance and direction.

The Writing Process

The process approach to writing involves many different kinds of writing and develops planning, composing and editing skills that are especially important to students learning the language of instruction.

- Assign writing tasks in a variety of formats, for different audiences and purposes.
- Organize production in specific stages: pre-writing, planning, drafts and revisions. Include the process in the evaluation scheme. Provide opportunities for practice and feedback before evaluation. Include peer-editing sessions and student-teacher conferences as part of the process.
- When responding to students' writing, do not point out every error. Instead, focus on identifying and explaining a consistent error so that the student can correct it.
- Be flexible. Requiring students to work through the entire process every time they write something will make writing a tedious chore. It is not necessary for students to polish all their work or to submit it for evaluation. Over the term, for example, you might invite them to develop three or four of their best pieces to hand in for evaluation.

Guided Research Projects

Introduce projects in a very structured way:

- Show students models of acceptable to outstanding projects, as well as ways of presenting information, such as posters, videos, comic books, interviews and roleplays, and traditional reports.
- Discuss the assessment criteria—the difference between satisfactory and excellent.
- Help students generate ideas. Group brainstorming works well for this.
- Help students develop pre-writing graphic organizers to organize their existing knowledge and indicate where research is needed.
- Teach research skills which may be unfamiliar to many students. Team up with the school librarian to design an introduction to the library.
- Teach students how to paraphrase. It is important not to penalize the errors of those who do paraphrase; if you do, they may revert to copying to ensure that their work is error-free.
- Provide constructive feedback on the process as well as the product. Base this assessment on your observations, as well as students' notes, journals and reading logs.
- Provide a checklist of steps to follow, along with timelines and due dates.
- Provide all the necessary resources—reference material, computers, presentation folders, paper, etc.—in order to eliminate economic advantages as a factor in evaluating the product.
- Review the process every time you assign a project. Be ready to give direct individualized instruction to students who need it.

Teaching Notes

These teaching notes offer suggestions for working with specific chapters of *My Country, Our History* and the reproducible activity pages that supplement the text.

The time required for each activity is not broken down; classes differ and schools have different ways of organizing the schedule of lessons. Organize the pace and sequence of activities to suit the timetable of the students at your school.

The teaching notes for each chapter of *My Country, Our History* are organized in two sections:

• *Features of the Text*: This section identifies specific linguistic and textual features that should be highlighted and explained during the directed reading process outlined in the introduction to this resource book. In some cases, this may occur during the

pre-reading stage; in others, it's more appropriate to deal with them during the reading or post-reading phases. In all cases, this section provides helpful suggestions and techniques for integrating a study of these features into a discussion of content.

• *Student Activities*: These notes provide practical—and specific—suggestions for organizing classroom activities and assignments that integrate language development with the major concepts or themes of each chapter.

In many cases, reproducible pages that can be photocopied and handed out to students are provided to accompany the activities. These are marked with an asterisk (*) and suggestions for using them are included in these notes.

Be Selective!

Your class probably includes students with different backgrounds, needs, interests and abilities. Some may have recently arrived in Canada, while others may have been born here. Some may still be learning English, while others may be proficient in the language. Some may be studying Canadian history for the first time, while others may have several years' experience with Canadian studies in the elementary and middle grades.

As a result, it is not necessary to "do" every suggested activity in this resource book with all the students. Select the activities that are appropriate for your class or for groups and individuals within it. For example, some students may not need to do some of the more structured writing activities. They may be ready for—and benefit more from engaging in—activities that encourage independence.

In addition, it is not necessary to use the materials exactly as suggested. Feel free to be creative in the way you tailor the activities to fit the backgrounds, needs, interests and abilities of the individual students in your class.

Chapter 1: What Is Canada?

Features of the Text

Subject-verb agreement

This chapter focuses on description, featuring present tense verbs. Point out models of subject-verb agreement, such as the following:

Many Canadians	*live*	in a few large cities...
The rest of the population	*lives*	all over Canada.
People in different parts of the country	*have*	different needs.
Southern Canada	*has*	a temperate climate.
There	*are*	some famous mountains in Canada.
There	*is*	good farmland along the St. Lawrence River...
Incomes	*are*	different in different parts of the country.
The average income in Canada *is*		one of the highest in the world.

Write some examples on the chalkboard and review the rule for subject-verb agreement: when the subject can be *he*, *she*, or *it*, add *-s* to present tense verbs.
Note: Be is the only verb that inflects for subject-verb agreement in the past tense: *was/were*.

Focus on this grammatical feature in responding to students' language use, but do not expect that all students will immediately become proficient at using it. It is one of the last-acquired features and it could be several years before all the ESL students have completely internalized it.

Language of spatial relationships

The chapter features many prepositional phrases indicating spatial relationships that are important in geography: *in the world, in the southeastern part of Canada, all over Canada, on three sides, to the east, to and from the ocean*, etc. Point out some of these and ask students to find other examples in specific paragraphs. Review the compass directions in English. Explain the locative phrases *located in* (¶1) and *surrounded by* (¶5); draw a picture to show the difference between *surrounding* and *surrounded by*.

Language of comparison: comparison of adjectives

This chapter makes many statements of comparison, using comparative and superlative forms of adjectives, especially in the discussion of charts and graphs. Review the rules for the formation of comparative and superlative forms of adjectives:

Add *-er*, *-est* to words of one syllable—*longer, colder, highest*. Double the final consonant in a consonant-vowel-consonant "sandwich"—*big-bigger*.
Change final *-y* to *-i* before adding *-er* or *-est*—*easy-easier*.
Use *more* and *the most* with words of more than two syllables—*the most multilingual*.

Use *many-more-(the) most* and *few-fewer-the fewest* with countable nouns—*more people, few Canadians, most cities*, etc.—and *much-more-(the) most* and *little-less-the least* with non-countable nouns—*more land, the most oil, less money, the least freedom*, etc.

Function of the colon

The colon is often used to introduce examples or an explanation of a concept or word: see ¶¶2, 3, 8, 29, 31. Explain that textbooks often use this technique to provide contextual support when new words or concepts are introduced. Suggest that students read on to find information explaining the word or concept, rather than stop to consult a dictionary.

Primary and secondary sources

Use the quotation from Chief Dan George (sidebar, p. 14) and the quotations from fugitive slaves on pp. 20-21 to develop the concept of primary and secondary sources and help students view history as an interpretation of available information rather than a collection of facts to be memorized.

Visual material

The illustrations should be viewed as part of the text, conveying important information that reinforces or supplements the printed text. For example, the photos on p. 15 provide a great deal of information about the people of Canada's First Nations that is not given in the printed text. To help students gain information from this kind of material, rather than view it merely as "decoration," try this strategy:

On pp. 11 and 12, guide the students through a discussion of the kinds of jobs they see by asking questions such as:
Do these jobs represent primary, manufacturing or service industries?
Where do you think the jobs might be located?
Which jobs do you think offer the highest salaries?
Which jobs would you prefer to have?
What kinds of jobs do you think you might have in the future?
Do you think you will work in the primary, manufacturing or service industries?

You could also bring in the classified section of a newspaper and invite students to classify some of the employment ads according to whether they represent primary, manufacturing or service industry jobs.

Student Activities

What Is Canada? *
Graphic organizer

Make a transparency of the organizer titled "What Is Canada?" and show it to the students before they read the chapter to give them an idea of the content and organization of the text. During or after reading, students can add specific information under each subheading. Encourage them to talk through the activity as they do it in groups.

Let Go of Your Dictionary! * *Reading strategy*	This activity helps students become less dependent on their dictionaries by showing them how much support for comprehension is provided in the text. Do one or two examples with the whole class, then encourage students to work together, "thinking aloud" to support each other's learning. When you take up the work, ask individual students questions like, "What word does your group have for this one?" This helps emphasize accountability in groupwork.
Similar or Different? * *Comparison chart*	Invite pairs of students to complete the comparison chart on Canada and another country. Students may choose their country of origin if they wish. Distribute the reproducible pages. Collect the written responses and record some of them on a classroom chart on the language of comparison.
Facts about Canada * *Vocabulary cloze*	Students apply the new words and demonstrate understanding of the material. Encourage students to discuss the activity in groups; call on individuals to read aloud specific sentences.
Suffixes That Mean "Someone Who..." * *Vocabulary study*	This activity introduces or reviews the concept of suffixes. You may need to remind some students of the rule for subject-verb agreement in the present tense. If this activity is assigned for homework, call on individuals to write sentences on the chalkboard the next day.
Canada: Facts and Figures * *Reading graphs and charts*	This activity focuses on the language needed to talk about information presented in graphs and charts.
Canada's First Nations: Contact * *Cause and effect*	Encourage students to read the passage independently and complete the cause-and-effect charts with a partner or in groups. Call on individual students to share their responses.
People of African Descent in Early Canada *Roleplay*	Read aloud the case study on p. 20 of the student's book and invite students to follow along in the text. Bring the material to life by suggesting that students use it to create a roleplay. Divide the class into groups of seven; six students are each responsible for giving a dramatic reading of one of the quotes from *The Refugee* in response to questions from the seventh student, who serves as an interviewer. The students can make up their own questions, or you could provide these:

What do you think of Canadian laws?
Is your life easier in Canada than it was in the United States?
Do you feel free in Canada?
Are you happy with your children's education in Canada?
Would you recommend immigrating to Canada to other people?
Do you think you would like to go back to the United States?

Each group can perform the roleplay for the class or for another group.

Supplementary Material

Case studies and interesting quotations are included in the body of the text of *My Country, Our History*, as well as in the sidebars. This material can be used in a variety of ways:

- Read it aloud to students.
- Encourage them to use it to create roleplays.
- Assign the material for independent reading at home, then invite students to follow up by writing journal responses.
- Organize small-group discussions based on the material.

The Story of Harriet Tubman*
Independent reading

Assign this activity for homework. At the beginning of the next class, provide time for students to check their homework with each other, while you do random checks to make sure that everyone in a group has done the homework. Make a transparency of the cloze sentences and call on individual students to read the sentences aloud. As you fill in the missing words, comment on the answers by saying things like, "Yes, in this sentence you need to use the noun," or "That's right, we need an adjective here," and so on. Write the label of the part of speech beside the sentence. Afterwards, point out three kinds of nouns in this passage: proper nouns (Harriet Tubman, Canada, the South); common nouns (slave, conductor, people); abstract nouns (freedom, slavery, danger). Emphasize that these labels are basic tools for language learning.

Collage

Invite students to work in groups to collect magazine pictures, newspaper photos and headlines, postcards, etc. that can be used to create a collage that represents what Canada means to them. Give each group time to explain its collage to the class or another group. On the chalkboard, record criteria for peer assessment and feedback, such as:

What did you like about their collage?
Did you understand the presentation?
What suggestions would you offer for next time?

Journal Responses

Students may choose one of these topics, or develop one of their own:

What I like (don't like) about living in Canada: Describe some of the things you really value about living in Canada, and a few of the things you would like to change.
Coming to Canada: When and why did you or your family come to Canada? Did (do) you and your family members feel welcome here? Why or why not? Do you think coming to Canada was a good idea? Why or why not?
Following Harriet Tubman: Imagine you are escaping from slavery in the United States. Harriet Tubman is guiding you and

your family to Canada. Write about your reasons for leaving or describe the journey or describe your hopes for the future.

Research   Refer students to ¶17 to find the origin of the word "Canada" and explain that many other place names also come from the languages of the peoples of Canada's First Nations; for example, Toronto, Ottawa, Athabasca, Kapuskasing and Nanaimo. Other place names, such as Red Deer and Medicine Hat, are English translations of Aboriginal place names. Give students a map of Canada or your community and invite them to make a list of place names they think may come from a First Nations language. Work with the librarian to provide reference material so that students can find the linguistic origins and meanings of some of these words.

Chapter 2: Canada Becomes a Country

Features of the Text

Latin vocabulary: the affix system

Although this chapter is shorter than Chapter 1, it is linguistically more complex. It introduces many words or new forms of familiar words that are made up of base words and affixes. This is an important feature of English—and of history, which often includes vocabulary that is abstract, complex and Latin-based. When they encounter what *seems* to be a new word, help students make the connection with known words. For example, you might say things like:

> You know that Canada used to be a British colony. What do you think a "colonist" is in ¶9?
> You know the meaning of "resource" because we talked about it in Chapter 1. Can you guess what a "resourceful" person is in ¶10?

Description and narration: simple past tense

Because this chapter contains descriptions of conditions and narration of events that occurred in the past, it is written almost entirely in the simple past tense. Review the pronunciation of regular past tense verbs that add -d or -ed (e.g., in ¶1, the past tense suffix is pronounced -d in "lived," but -t in "worked"; in ¶3, the past tense suffix is pronounced as -id in "defeated" and "ended"). Ask students to point out examples of irregular past tense verbs (e.g., "became," "was," "had," "made" in ¶1). Remind them that when talking or writing about the past in English, we mark the past tense on every verb. This is not the case in some other languages: ask students about their languages. For example, some languages show tense by using an adverbial phrase such as "in 1956" rather than inflecting the verbs.

Problems and solutions: speculation and hypothesis

Paragraphs 14-18 feature "the future in the past" (speculation in the past about the future), using modals to express possibility (what might or would happen; e.g., what *might happen* when the free trade agreement ended, how Confederation *would help* the economy). To help show how this is different from the future tense, invite students to explain what they thought Canada *would be* like before they *came* here.

Student Activities

What Do We Know about Colonization?* Pre-reading activity

Use this interactive task to activate students' previous experience or knowledge of the abstract concepts of "colonization" and "independence." The activity also provides opportunities for students to talk to each other, getting to know students from other groups and learn about each other's countries.

Call on individuals to read aloud their statements about the information. Invite students from former colonies to talk about how their country became independent and when and how it celebrates

19

independence. If there are students from Hong Kong in the class, invite them to talk about the transfer of the colony back to China.

Canada Becomes a Country*
Graphic organizer

This organizer helps students see the more complex organization of ideas in this chapter. Explain that Chapter 2 is about Britain's colonies in North America and how Canada became a nation. After surveying the chapter, distribute the organizer and instruct students to compare it with the guiding questions in the chapter. They can complete it as you guide the reading of each section.

More Suffixes That Mean "Someone Who..."*
Vocabulary study

This is an extension of the work on suffixes that began in Chapter 1. Questions 1 and 2 can be assigned for homework. Students may need class time to interview other students in the class or in the school to complete Question 3.

The Affix System*
Vocabulary study

Read the explanation with the students, then assign the task as a group activity. Make a transparency and call on individuals to fill in some of the words. Parts of this activity can become a quiz in the next class.

Jigsaw Word Puzzle*
Review

This interactive puzzle helps students review vocabulary and concepts related to Confederation.

Divide students into groups of four and give each group member one of the jigsaw puzzle sheets. The solutions are the same, but each student has a different set of clues. To solve the puzzle, group members must work together.

Note: All four clues may not be needed for every word. To ensure that no student is always the one with the last piece of information, rotate the starting turns; i.e., for the first word, the student with sheet A reads the first clue; for the second word, the student with sheet B begins; and so on. The answer key is on p. 217.

Wishes, Hopes, Plans, Fears and Worries...*
Sentence completion

This activity provides support or a "scaffold" for the students' writing. The focus is the language of "future in the past," using modal and conditional verbs.

Note: In many languages, the structure is different. For example, the colonists' thoughts and feelings might be expressed as "they were afraid that when the free trade agreement will end, they will not be able to sell their goods in America." Ask students how their languages express thoughts, feelings and speech that took place in the past but were about the future in relation to that past time.

Writing Scaffolds

Writing scaffolds are frameworks that support the students' writing. Cloze activities, sentence completion exercises and paragraph frames are examples of scaffolds that provide the kind of structure many students need when they are beginning to write.

As they become more proficient at producing sentences and paragraphs of specific types, these supports are gradually removed.

The Fathers of Confederation*
Queen Victoria*
Guided research

This is a jigsaw research assignment. Follow these steps:

- Refer students to the photograph of John A. Macdonald on p. 27 and the photograph of the fathers of Confederation on p. 29. Tell them that all Canadians know the names of some of the key figures in Confederation.
- Give every student a copy of the outline on Macdonald and discuss it as a model for gathering information for a research project.
- Organize the class in jigsaw groups of three. Give each student in the group a different research assignment — on George-Etienne Cartier, George Brown or Queen Victoria. Their task is to find the missing information.
- Arrange for the librarian to present a simple introduction to using reference material in the school's resource centre.
- Be available to help students find the information they need to complete their outlines. They may do this individually or with partners from other groups who are researching the same topic.
- Once back in the classroom, invite students to work alone, with a partner or with a small "expert group" to create a poster or other display of information about the historical figure they researched.
- When finished, students return to their original jigsaw groups. Each student in the group then takes the other two group members to her or his poster, hands out copies of the original blank outline, and makes a brief oral presentation so that the other group members can complete the chart as a guided listening activity, asking questions for clarification as necessary. Organize the rotation so that only one group is at a poster at one time.
- Provide criteria for peer evaluation of the presentation — the effectiveness of the poster, the clarity of the presentation and the interest level.

Field trip and co-operative project

This activity offers a valuable opportunity for students, especially newcomers, to develop a first-hand understanding of what life was like for early settlers in Canada.

- Organize a trip to a museum house or settlement in your area.
- Before the trip, collect books and pictures that can be used to stimulate interest and develop students' background knowledge.
- Announce the field trip. Remember that an instructional field trip may be a new experience for some students from other countries. Explain that it is an important part of the program and that a learning task is involved. Explain this, too, in the permission letters you send home to parents. Make sure the letters are in a language that parents can

21

understand. Some of the students, or others in the school, may be able to translate the letter.

- Show students the books and pictures, and invite comments and questions.
- Organize students into groups of three or four and assign a specific topic to each group: e.g., homes and furniture, food and cooking, farming methods, trades and crafts, etc. Suggest that students who would benefit from a more challenging assignment research social relationships.
- Instruct each group to prepare questions about the assigned topic and collect information on the topic during the trip. Check to make sure that every group member has a specific responsibility and has prepared a set of questions.
- Enjoy the trip! It's a good idea to make groups of students responsible for each other so that it isn't necessary to monitor them constantly. Take along a Polaroid camera so you can snap the students in action.
- When you return to class, give each group its own set of photos. They can use these photos, as well as postcards, fact sheets, and the resources you collected, to prepare a group presentation or display for the class. Spend time helping each group organize its material and choose the most effective way of presenting it. Plan a "dry run" if it's to be an oral presentation. Invite parents to see the presentation or display, or encourage each student to invite a student or teacher from another class.

Writing Questions

It's often helpful to provide model questions beginning with question words to demonstrate the use of the auxiliary verb *did*. Here are some examples:

What tools did they use?
When did the first settlers arrive in _____?
Where did they come from?
How did they remove the trees?
Why did they build walls and fences?

Note: No auxiliary verb is used when "who" is the subject (e.g., Who looked after the chickens?).

Journal responses

The field trip: Encourage students to respond to the field trip by asking questions such as:

What did you learn?
What did you like or find interesting?
What was the best part?
Did anything surprise you?

A letter home: Invite students to imagine they are settlers writing a letter to a relative in their home country. Suggest that they describe their daily lives and report whether they're glad they decided to come to Canada.

Time travel: Encourage students to imagine they are settlers who, by accident, have arrived in the future. Invite them to describe their reactions to their new environment.

Timeline

Make a timeline of significant events in your own life and show it to students. Suggest that they interview each other in pairs and create timelines for each other. Using a large sheet of squared chart paper, make a timeline for Canada. Start with "10 000 years ago: the First Nations peoples were here" and mark Confederation and the current year. Add more events as you work through the textbook and as major events occur during the school year.

Students may find it interesting to work in groups or with a partner to create timelines for their home countries, choosing their own starting point and marking significant events — important dynasties or rulers, inventions, wars, invasions, revolutions, nationhood, etc.

Chapter 3: Expansion of the Country: 1867-1885

Features of the Text

Passive voice

This chapter introduces passive verbs, which are highlighted in the text. During the post-reading stage, refer students to sections that contain examples of verbs in the passive voice and explain why this voice is used. For example:

¶9   To maintain "settlers" as the subject.

¶20   We don't know or it doesn't matter exactly who did this.

¶27   The process (building) and the product (the railway) are the focus of the text, not the people who did it.

p. 44   "Case Study: The Chinese": Passive voice is often used in "were not treated well" if we don't know—or want to avoid saying—exactly who was responsible.

      Give some more examples:

      Where were you born?

      When was this school built?

      What is paper made of?

      What is grown in the Prairies?

      Why was the Great Wall of China built?

      How were the Pyramids of Egypt built?

Passive Verbs in Academic Text

Passive verbs, which are used infrequently in most day-to-day inter-actions, are very common in academic text, especially when the focus is on a process, a product or a result, rather than on the people carrying out the process, producing the product, or causing the result. Here are some examples from other disciplines:

Science: The water was heated to 100°C.

Geography: Wheat is grown on the prairies.

Mathematics: This amount is subtracted...

Encourage students to check other texts to find more examples.

Threats, plans, promises and hopes in the past

This chapter includes several examples of "future in the past" conditional verbs used to express threats, plans and promises. For example:

¶8   Riel and the Métis would not join Confederation. They would fight the Canadian government.

¶10   The Canadian government would also give money...

      Point out the use of this alternative structure for indicating plans and promises:

¶10   The Métis were to get half a million hectares of land...

More verbs indicating hopes, plans and promises using "would" are found in ¶¶23, 24, 26, 28, 30 and 31.

Affixes	This chapter expands the use of Latin vocabulary and word families.

Student Activities

Decisions, Decisions... ⋆ *Graphic organizer*	This organizer focuses on decision-making: weighing the advantages and disadvantages of joining Confederation. Before they read, show students the organizer to help orient them to the chapter. Students can fill it in as they finish reading the relevant sections of text.
Expansion of the Country ⋆ *Reading strategy*	This activity requires students to interpret the text and support their inferences. Emphasize that copying verbatim does not demonstrate comprehension!
Conflicts and Solutions ⋆ *Recognizing key concepts*	This activity helps students focus on a key concept in the study of history at the same time as they practise finding main ideas and examples in a text. Encourage them to refer to the text to locate the information they need to complete this chart.
More Affixes! ⋆ *Vocabulary study*	Read the explanation with the students, then brainstorm to come up with a list of other words they know that use some of these affixes. Encourage students to review the material on affixes from Chapters 1 and 2 before they start the cloze activity. They may work together or independently to complete this task. Make a transparency and invite individuals to fill in some of the words. Instruct students to learn the affixes and re-use some items from the activity sheet in a quiz.
	Encourage students to start a vocabulary notebook to record new words and word families. From time to time, set aside a few minutes of class time for students to update their notebooks, and check them regularly.
Expansion of the Country ⋆ *Crossword puzzle*	This puzzle, which is based on the content of the text and the information on affixes, is designed for partners. One partner has the Down clues, while the other has the Across clues.
Canada Grows ⋆ *Cloze—passive verbs*	This activity provides structured practice in using passive verbs. Read the explanation with the students, then make a transparency of the activity sheets and invite students to supply the verbs. Distribute copies for group or individual practice, or for homework. Items from the activity sheets can be re-used in a quiz.
The Métis Want Some Guarantees ⋆ *Roleplay*	In groups of five, students read the roleplay between Riel and the Métis. Then, invite each group to write a script for a discussion that might have taken place between representatives of the Métis and the Canadian government. Once they have rehearsed their parts, students perform their roleplay for the class. The focus is on the language of requests, demands and promises.

Promises,
Promises... *
Paragraph frame

Journal responses

This scaffolded writing activity focuses on paragraph structure: main idea, examples and concluding statement. The content revisits the major theme of the chapter.

Conflict of values: This chapter describes the conflict between the values of the First Nations peoples and the Europeans. They believed in different things and wanted to live very different kinds of lives. Encourage students to write a journal response about a conflict of values in their own lives. Help them get started by asking questions like:

> Do you ever find that your ideas or values are in conflict with the ideas of others? For example, do you have exactly the same values as all your friends? As your teachers? As your classmates? As your parents? Do these differences create conflict?

Building the railway: You are a Chinese worker building the railway. Write a letter home describing the work, the working conditions and the way your co-workers and bosses treat you. Write about your wishes and dreams for the future and ask about your family.

Chapter 4: Settlement of the West

Features of the Text

Cause-and-effect words and phrases

This chapter features many cause-and-effect statements. During the post-reading stage, refer students to the text to find examples such as the following and identify (distinguish between) the cause and the effect in each statement. Help the class with the first few, then assign the rest as a group activity.

¶2	This meant
¶3	Because the National Policy
¶6	One cause
¶7	led to
	because
¶8	led to
	As a result of
¶9	source of
	Therefore
	For all these reasons
¶10	for three reasons
¶13	because of
¶14	the result of
¶16	This made
¶22	in order to
¶27	why
¶28	because
¶30	As a result of
¶35	some of the reasons
¶38	due to
	so...that

Because...Because of...

"Because" introduces a verb phrase about a cause.
"Because of" introduces a noun phrase about a cause.
"As a result of" introduces a noun phrase about a cause. Students looking at the word "result" may be misled into believing the phrase introduces the result, especially because the expression "as a result" *does* introduce a statement about a result!

Student Activities

Settlement of the West* Graphic organizer

This organizer focuses on conflict and conflict resolution. Use it before reading to show students how the text is organized. Students can fill in the information after they read, revisiting appropriate sections of text to check details.

Let Go of Your Dictionary! *Reading strategy*	This activity helps students discover that a text often contains many clues to the meaning of unfamiliar words. Begin the activity in class, then suggest that students finish it for homework.
Greek and Latin Roots *Vocabulary study*	This lesson on word analysis introduces information on common word roots, using words the students have already encountered in the text. Distribute the reference sheets and assign the activity sheet for homework. Encourage students to learn a set of words and recognize the general meaning of the common element, rather than memorize the roots alone. Make sure that students continue to keep vocabulary notebooks, including various forms of a new word: noun, verb, etc., as well as derivatives formed by adding prefixes or suffixes. Some of these items can be re-used in a quiz.

A Note about Pronunciation

Some dictionaries use the diacritical mark (') to indicate that the *following* syllable is stressed, while others use it to indicate that the stress is on the *preceding* syllable. Thus, in one dictionary, 'rebel, for example, may be shown as the noun while re'bel is the verb. This is the system used in the word list on p. 103. In another dictionary, the situation may be reversed. Warn students to check the system used in the dictionary they are referring to.

Many words (e.g., 'ancestor, an'cestral) change the main stress when affixes are added. Say these words aloud so that students can hear the shift in stress and use choral repetition to provide pronunciation practice.

Settlement of the West *Reading strategy*	This activity focuses on the elements of the most common paragraph structure in English: topic sentence, consisting of a general statement; evidence, details or examples, sometimes introduced by phrases such as "first of all," "in addition," "also," etc.; and, sometimes, a concluding summary. When students are skimming to get a general idea of the content of a text, suggest that they focus on the generalizations only, leaving the details for a second reading.
Past and More Past *Grammar practice*	English verb tenses cause problems for many ESL learners. This activity helps them understand the time relationships expressed when both the simple past and the past perfect tense are used.
The Trial of Louis Riel *Roleplay*	Invite students to work in groups of five to read the script and act as a jury to determine Riel's guilt or innocence. Explain that a jury at a criminal trial normally consists of 12 people, but their juries will be smaller to give everyone more opportunity to speak.
Canadians in Conflict *Jigsaw activity*	Organize students in groups of four and give each group member a different biography to read to the group. Circulate as students rehearse, helping with pronunciation, pacing, etc.

The Alberta Homesteader* Poetry	Introduce the poem by telling students that it is about the life of a settler in the West. Suggest that they listen to the poem and decide whether this settler is glad he accepted the government's offer of free land. Why do they think so?
	Read the poem aloud and invite responses. Distribute copies and read the poem aloud again. Encourage students to discuss the poem in small groups, preparing questions for you about words or ideas they don't understand. Each group could also rehearse one verse for choral reading.
Coming to Canada* Journal responses	Encourage students to choose some of the suggested topics and write several journal entries about their own arrival in Canada. Students who were born in Canada may choose to interview classmates, using the same questions, and write either a biographical account or a personal response to their classmates' experiences.
Independent reading	Students will enjoy reading about the experiences of teenagers arriving in Canada and adapting to a new way of life. *New Canadian Voices* (Jessie Porter, ed. Wall and Emerson: Toronto) is a collection of writing by ESL students at Jarvis Collegiate in Toronto.
Research	This activity makes an excellent follow-up to the material on word origins. Invite students to research the origins of their own languages.

> Which language family does your home language belong to? What languages is it related to?
> What words has your language "borrowed" from other languages? Are there any English words in your language?
> What writing system does your language use (e.g., an alphabet, a syllabary, or a set of characters representing ideas rather than sounds)?

Students can get most of this information from their parents or a member of the community. In addition, most encyclopedias will have this information and *The Cambridge Encyclopedia of Language* is also a useful source. Students might also be interested in finding out about the languages of the peoples of Canada's First Nations.

Chapter 5: Working in Canada 1867-1913

Features of the Text

Cause and effect, description

The first part of this chapter (¶¶1-7 and the case study) consists of a series of cause-and-effect statements. The second part is more descriptive and easier to read, even though it is longer. As a result, the graphic organizers for this chapter treat the two parts separately, representing the concepts in different ways.

Idioms

Discuss these idiomatic expressions during the directed reading process:

Introduction — turn of the century
Case study — the rise of
¶14 to get ahead
    laid off
¶16 on the job
¶17 room and board
¶19 take advantage of
¶24 locked them out
    at the first hint of
¶26 live-in servants
    on call
¶29 open to women
    under pressure

About Idioms

Idioms exist in every language. They add colour and expressiveness to our language, especially speech. However, they are not the same across languages and cultures. For example, while English speakers may complain of "a frog in the throat," the equivalent expression in French translates into English as "a cat in the throat."

ESL students who are unfamiliar with English idioms often try to translate them literally. If you use expressions such as, "Now we're cookin'," or "Take a stab at it!" to encourage students, those who don't know the figurative meanings will be very surprised!

Pay attention to these expressions when they crop up in class or in text passages. Rephrase them so that students can attach meaning to them, and post a list of the week's idioms on your bulletin board. Because using idiomatic language makes them sound more like fluent native speakers, language learners enjoy adding these to their repertoire.

Past participles as adjective phrases

In English, the past participle can function as an adjective. Point out some of these examples from the chapter:

¶2 American-made products
¶4 manufactured goods

¶5 Towns...were located...
¶6 resource-based industries
   the water needed for paper making
Case study — products made in their own country
¶9 crowded...conditions
¶10 many houses were poorly built
¶12 the causes...were still unknown
¶13 Once these conditions were controlled
¶16 injured workers
¶22 skilled workers
¶24 increased costs
   Sometimes workers became...frustrated

Reduced Relative Clauses

The adjectival past participle is often derived from a reduced relative clause. "Unpacking" a few examples of these will help students understand the meaning of this very dense syntactic form. For example, "manufactured goods" can be understood as a condensed form of...

goods   that   had been manufactured
                  ↑   ↑
          relative pronoun   *passive verb*

Similarly, a phrase such as "the water needed" is a reduced form of "the water that was needed" and "resource-based industries" is a reduced form of "industries that were based on resources" and so on.

Student Activities

The Growth of Cities: 1867-1913* Graphic organizer

This organizer shows the development of concepts in ¶¶1-7 and in the case study that follows. Invite students to look at the organizer before reading and make predictions about the information they are likely to find in the text. They can fill in the organizer as they read ¶¶1-7.

Using the Graphic Organizer* Cause-and-effect statements

This activity requires students to write cause-and-effect statements relating to the material in ¶¶1-7, based on the information in the graphic organizer.

Living and Working in Canada* Graphic organizer

This "attributes map" represents the major concepts introduced in the description of living and working conditions in rural and urban Canada between 1867 and 1913. Invite students to look at the map before reading this section, then add details after reading each sub-section. The pre-reading questions at the beginning of each sub-section will help alert them to the information to look for as they read.

31

Using the Graphic Organizer* Paragraph scaffold	Using information from the attributes map and referring to the chapter if necessary, students can use the scaffold to develop a paragraph that makes a general statement followed by supporting examples. The term "topic sentence" is introduced. Suggest that students write one paragraph and submit it for feedback, then produce another that will be evaluated formally (e.g., as a homework assignment or in an open-book test).
Expanding Your Vocabulary* Cloze	Suggest that students refer to the text to find the words, or alternative forms of the words, in context, then use the words or alternative forms in the sentences.
What Do You See?* Photo analysis	This activity helps students use visual information provided in texts. Use the questions to guide discussion in groups. The cloze activity provides a model of a written description. Suggest that each student choose another photograph and write a description. This writing assignment provides an excellent opportunity to use the writing process, including peer-response groups.
Children at Work* Well, You Just Worked Hard...* Children of the Factory* Writing questions	This activity involves students in learning more about working conditions in Canada in the second half of the 19th century. At the same time, it provides them with an opportunity to practise formulating question-word questions (using what, where, when, why and how). Read the first passage with the whole class and point out the patterns. For example:

What age	are	you?
What ages	are	they?
↑	↑	↑
question word	+ "be" +	subject

Where	do	you	work?
What hours	do	you	work?
What age	would	you	be...?
How long	have	you	been working...?
↑	↑	↑	↑
question word	+ auxiliary +	subject +	the rest of the verb

Women Who Made a Difference* Problem-solving	This activity raises students' awareness of the role of women in Canadian history. Divide students into groups of three and give each group member one of the mini-biographies to read and talk about with others in the group. Then, distribute the assignment and give the groups a specified period to choose and name their project. Call on a student from each group to announce the group's decision and explain the reasons for the choices.
Equality for Canadian Women* Paragraph structure	This activity, which is based on the material in the biographies of Stowe, Youmans and Denison, gives students more practice in writing topic sentences and providing supporting ideas.

32

Journal responses

Invite students to write a descriptive piece about work and working conditions. For example, suggest that they describe the following:

Describe a job you have had or that you have now.
Describe a job you would like to have.
Describe a job you would hate to have.
Describe working conditions for adults or children in another country.

Chapter 6: Canada and World War I: 1914-1921

Features of the Text

Suffixes

This chapter provides a number of opportunities to expand students' awareness of common suffixes. Point out examples after students have completed reading the whole chapter.

- Words ending in "-ism," meaning a belief or ideology, as in ¶3: nationalism, imperialism, militarism. Invite students to think of other "-isms" that describe political or religious ideologies. These words are common to many languages.
- Words ending in "-ist," meaning a supporter or believer (e.g., "nationalists" in ¶8, "suffragists" in ¶38, "prohibitionists" in Question a on p. 85, "capitalists" in ¶55 and "communists" in ¶56).

Adjectival participles

This chapter includes more examples of the past participle used as an adjective:

¶1   Canadians were surprised...
¶2   all the major countries were involved...
¶5   European countries became worried...
¶6   Allied Powers
¶11 unemployed
¶13 poorly trained and equipped
¶14 barbed wire
¶50 deeply divided, dissatisfied, disappointed
¶51 no longer needed
¶52 dissatisfied, rejected, unappreciated, bored, frustrated, humiliated
¶59 Farmers were upset...
¶60 they felt betrayed...

Bored or Boring?

ESL students sometimes have trouble understanding when to use the past participle and present participle of "emotive verbs" as adjectives (e.g., bored—boring, surprised—surprising, etc.). Provide some examples, such as the following, that show the difference in meaning:

If I teach an interesting lesson, you feel interested.
If you have to read a boring book, you feel bored.
If your lunch is satisfying, you feel satisfied.
If the homework is frustrating, you feel frustrated.

Cause and effect, description

Many of the ideas in this chapter are causally related (e.g. ¶¶1-12 How did Canada become involved in the war?). The chapter also includes a number of descriptive passages (e.g., ¶¶14-18 What was a soldier's life like?). Suggestions for using these sections are offered in the material that follows (see the graphic organizers).

Student Activities

How Do You Feel about War?*
Class survey

This pre-reading activity encourages students to draw on their previous experience and explore their own attitudes to war. Many students from other countries have experienced war personally and some young men have been conscripted into the armed forces. Be sensitive to the reluctance of some students to discuss their experiences: make the activity optional and provide these students with an alternative task. For example, some may be willing to share their ideas and experiences in a journal entry that only you will see, or you might provide some visual material on World War I for them to look at.

As a follow-up to a reading of this chapter, invite students to revisit their surveys and estimate how many people in the class would have supported Canada's involvement in World War I, and how many would not.

Canada and World War I*
Graphic organizer

This pre-reading organizer shows students the aspects or components of the topic that are included in this chapter. You can also use the organizer as a guide for assigning tasks based on the organizers provided for various sections of the chapter (see the following material).

How Did Canada Become Involved in the War?*
Graphic organizer

This cloze activity focuses on expressions of cause and effect about the information in ¶¶1-12.

Canadians at War in Europe*
Supporting the War at Home*
The Political Situation at Home*
Graphic organizers

Organize the class for a jigsaw reading and discussion activity:

- Divide students into groups of three.
- Assign a different section of the chapter to each student in the group and give each the organizer for the appropriate section. (*Note:* "The Political Situation at Home" is the most demanding assignment; "Supporting the War at Home" is less demanding.)
- Students work together in expert groups with students from other groups who have been assigned the same topic.
- When students have completed the organizer accurately, instruct them to plan how they will use it to help guide other students through this section of text. Give each student enough copies of the organizer to take back to her or his jigsaw group.
- Students return to their jigsaw groups and guide the other group members through the text, using the organizer.
- Students check the organizers for accuracy.

The End of the War*
Transparency

Make a transparency of this sheet to guide the students in reading, thinking and discussing this short, but important, section of the text.

After the War*
Graphic organizer

Invite students to complete this organizer during or after reading the last section of text. This activity could be assigned for homework.

Canada and World War I*
Vocabulary development

This activity provides practice in inferring word meanings from context. The cloze segment of the activity helps reinforce major concepts and vocabulary. Some of the terms can be re-used in a quiz or test.

Conscription Crossfire*
Letters to the editor

Invite pairs of students to adopt the point of view of either a French Canadian opposed to Canada's involvement in the war or an English Canadian who supports it. Make sure all students understand the format of a formal letter. When students have finished a first draft, encourage them to read each other's letters, commenting on the strength of the arguments presented. Then, instruct them to consider the comments and revise their letters accordingly.

War films

Select excerpts from films such as *Paths of Glory, All Quiet on the Western Front* and *I Think of You Often* that show the living and fighting conditions for soldiers in World War I. Provide viewing directions that encourage students to focus on specific aspects of the film; for example, sense impressions of trench warfare or the emotional content of a scene.

Canadian War Poetry*
Reading poetry

Read the poems aloud and initiate a class discussion focusing on questions such as, Why did the poets write these poems? What is their point of view? How are the poems different in style and format? Emphasize that it is not necessary to understand every word in order to understand the message and appreciate the poet's use of language.

Journal responses

Letters: Invite students to choose one of the following tasks:

> You are a soldier or nurse at the front. Write a letter home, describing conditions and how you are now feeling about the war, and communicating your love.
> A member of your family is a soldier or a nurse at the front. Write a letter to this relative, trying to encourage optimism about the progress of the war, describing how you are supporting the war effort at home, and communicating your love.

Research project

The First World War offers many opportunities for introducing research assignments, which can be completed individually or with a partner or small group. Remember that many students who have been educated in other countries have little experience with projects such as this: see p. 11 in the introduction to this resource book for suggestions for introducing students to this important skill. After showing the students some model projects and discussing the evaluation criteria, generate ideas for topics, provide a checklist of the steps to follow, and specify time lines for completing each step.

Chapter 7: Good Times and Bad in the 1920s and 1930s

Features of the Text

Contrasting ideas, cause and effect

As the title indicates, this chapter covers two contrasting major ideas: good times and bad. The chapter is structured so that it deals with the causes and effects of prosperity in the 1920s, then the causes and effects of the Depression in the 1930s.

Idioms

This chapter includes a number of idiomatic expressions that may be unfamiliar to ESL learners. Point out one or two of these and explain them, using the word "idiom" in your explanation. For example:

¶21 went downhill
¶23 went broke

The student activities include a task focusing on these expressions (see "Good Times and Bad" in the Student Activities).

Student Activities

Good Times and Bad in the 1920s and 1930s* Graphic organizer

Use this organizer to create a transparency that can be shown to the students to give them an overview of the content of the chapter. It will help them see the parallel cause-and-effect structure and understand the overall organization of the text before they start to read.

Boom and Bust: Good Times* Boom and Bust: Bad Times* What Would Happen if...?* Pre-reading activity

These activities help develop some of the concepts relating to "boom" and "bust" that are important to understanding the causal relationships in this chapter. The writing activity focuses on using transition words to link contrasting ideas. It's a good idea to highlight the sentence pattern expressing condition, which is often used to speculate about cause and effect.

$$If + \quad past\ tense \quad + \quad conditional$$

If Canadians had little or no money, they would probably put their money in the bank.

Condition   *Probable result*

We're Rich!* How the stock market works

Make transparencies of the cartoon sequence, "We're Rich!," to illustrate how the stock market works. Use the cartoons before reading ¶¶7-9. As a follow-up, invite students to create their own cartoon sequence about what a family might do with money made on the stock market.

Help students understand that the economy was operating on credit. Ask them this question:

Where do you think people got the money to buy shares?

Students may also be interested in discussing this question:

All Canadians pay federal and provincial sales taxes on nearly everything they buy. Should the government collect taxes on banking services or the buying and selling of shares?

Living on Easy Street*
Graphic organizer

This chart can be used after reading ¶¶10-16 to help students practise checking details relating to cause and effect, as well as supporting an opinion. Call on individual students to make oral statements about the chart, expressing cause-and-effect relationships and opinion.

Buy, Buy, Buy!*
Creating a radio commercial

Organize students into groups for this activity. Encourage them to listen to some radio commercials and talk about some of the techniques they hear, such as jingles, repetition, rhyme, music, sound effects, etc. Show students how to use the checklist to evaluate their own work and that of their peers.

How Did the Great Depression Affect the Lives of Canadians?*
Graphic organizer

Students can use this during or after reading ¶¶26-39 to evaluate the effects of the Depression on the lives of Canadians. Encourage groups to develop a paragraph about one of the topics, consisting of a generalization and two or three examples. Post the paragraphs so that students can read each other's work.

Good Times and Bad*
Idioms

Encourage students to refer to the text to find the idioms and infer their meaning from the context.

All about Economics*
Crossword puzzle

This puzzle requires students to refer to the text to check word meanings in context. Students can complete this activity in pairs; one student has the Across clues and the other has the Down clues.

Dear Prime Minister Bennett...
Letter-writing

Invite students to choose one of these roles—a child, a single man, an immigrant, a farmer or a worker—and write to Prime Minister Bennett, using the letter on p. 104 as a model. Encourage them to include some of the following ideas:

- How the effects of the Depression have changed your life.
- How the Depression has changed your thoughts and feelings about friends, family, money, buying products and employment.
- Why you need help.
- How the government can help you.

Reading aloud

Reading aloud excerpts from Barry Broadfoot's oral history, *Ten Lost Years*, is an excellent way to stimulate a sense of the times.

Journal responses
Responding to the photographs

Encourage students to write a descriptive piece based on one of the photographs in this chapter, choosing the point of view of either an observer or one of the people in the picture. Remind them to include both what they see and what they feel. The following photos are particularly rich in information:

p. 102 The evicted family
p. 103 The women sewing or the men on the relief project
p. 109 The men's camp

Talking about racism

Issues of racism, prejudice and discrimination are important in the lives of most immigrant students, as well as North American and European history. The material on pp. 105-106 and the case study on pp. 113-114 can stimulate whole-class or small-group discussion of these issues. This theme is important in Chapter 8 and recurs in later chapters as well.

For example, once the students have read ¶¶31-34, you might initiate a discussion by saying something like:

> Look at the first picture on p. 105. Who sent the letter? What do you think the writers are threatening to do? What do you think the person who received this letter may have done to make the writers angry? What would you do if you received a letter like this? Is it legal to send letters like this?
>
> Look at the second photo on p. 105. Who are these people? Why are they dressed like this? What do you think the cross symbolizes? What do they want? Would this meeting be legal in Canada today? Do you think there are people today who share some of the ideas of the Ku Klux Klan? Are there people in this school who share some of these ideas? How do you know? What do you think we should do about it?

Read aloud the case study on pp. 113-114. Don't be surprised if some students whose roots are in continents other than Europe or North America have limited knowledge of the Holocaust, or of European history in general. Encourage students to ask questions and discuss the photographs by saying something like:

> Look at the photograph on p. 113. Who are these people? Where do you think they are from? Why do they have numbers on their arms?
>
> Now look at the photo on p. 114. These people did not survive. Why were they killed? Do you think Canada should have allowed Jewish refugees to come here during the Second World War?

As a follow-up, invite a representative of your school board's race and ethno-cultural equity program or a school anti-racism group to visit the class and talk to students.

Chapter 8: Canada and World War II: 1939-1945

Features of the Text

This chapter is organized in six major sections:

How Canada became involved in the war: ¶¶1-19 (cause and effect).

How Canadians felt about the war: ¶¶20-29 (cause and effect, sequence).

Canadians at war in Europe and Asia: ¶¶24-38 (sequence of events).

Supporting the war at home: ¶¶39-44 (cause and effect, description).

How the war changed Canadian society: ¶¶45-53 (cause and effect).

The political and economic effects of the war: ¶¶54-end (cause and effect, sequence).

As you work through the chapter with the students, you will notice that the text is becoming increasingly complex. The chapters are longer, with some subtopics extending over more than one page. New words continue to be introduced and the sentence patterns are more varied. It is important to continue to guide the students' reading of the text so that they get the most out of it.

Colon and semicolon

This chapter contains a number of instances (e.g., ¶¶3, 9) in which the colon is used to introduce an explanation or an elaboration of a word or idea.

In addition, it contains a number of instances (e.g., ¶¶6, 10) in which the semicolon is used to link items in a list or to show that ideas or events are parallel or causally or sequentially related.

Quotation marks

Point out the use of quotation marks as a technique employed by writers to distance themselves from the ideas they are describing (e.g., ¶28: race, inferior; ¶52 and case study on p.p. 136-137: enemy aliens).

Student Activities

Canada and World War II*
Graphic organizer

This organizer, which is designed to be used before students start reading, provides an overview of the chapter. Instruct students to turn to the table of contents for this chapter and record the questions under the appropriate headings on the organizer. As they read the text and find the answers, they can check the questions in the organizer.

From One World War to Another*
Chart

This is a matching exercise using information from ¶¶5-16.

The Causes of World War II*
Paragraph frame

This activity helps students construct effective paragraphs and organize them into a group essay. It works best when students have access to computers to create, compile and edit their work. If each group prints its work one paragraph to a page, using a large font, the essays can be posted for display. Students can then look at each other's work, noting differences in phrasing.

Should We Go to War Again? *
Paraphrasing

This sentence completion activity provides students with structured practice in paraphrasing main points from the text, ¶¶20-22.

Should We Go to War Again? *
Group discussion

Use the graphic symbol of the scale to stimulate group discussion. Call on an individual from each group to report the group's decision.

Allons-y Canadiens!
Canadians at War in Europe and Asia *
Allons-y Canadiens!
Supporting the War at Home *
Graphic organizers

Divide the class in half and distribute one of these organizers to each half. Organize the students into small groups and instruct them to read the appropriate sections of the text and complete their organizers in preparation for the next activity. Circulate among the groups, encouraging individual students to tell you what they have discovered.

Creating a newsreel

This is an opportunity for half the class to prepare a newsreel presentation on Canadians at war in Europe and Asia while the other half prepares a newsreel on supporting the war at home.

- Begin by showing students some actual newsreel footage of the war to give them a sense of style and content.
- Within each topic, organize small groups to prepare different segments, using the organizer as a guide to the content.
- Discuss the roles students might play when they create their presentations (e.g., announcers, interviewers, factory and farm workers, industrialists, scientists, personnel in the armed forces, politicians, etc.).
- Encourage students to carry out the planning and organization while you provide advice, props and material, music and time lines. Consult your drama department or teacher for advice and assistance.
- Groups can present their newsreels live or on videotape.
- After their presentation, students may distribute copies of their organizer for other students to fill in or use as a study guide at home.

How the War Changed Canadian Society *
The Political and Economic Effects of the War *
Graphic organizers

Instruct students to complete these organizers during or after independent reading in class or for homework. Take up the organizers next day, calling on individuals to contribute specific points under each heading and filling in the information on a transparency.

41

Let Go of Your
*Dictionary!**
Vocabulary

Distribute the flow chart illustrating how to deal with new vocabulary. Then read aloud short sections of text, "thinking aloud" as you go, to model the process of decoding word meaning from the context. Here are some examples of the kinds of things you might say:

¶26 "Hitler called this action '*blitzkrieg*' or 'lightning war.'"
I don't need to look up "*blitzkrieg*" because the meaning is given right after it—"lightning war."
¶28 "The Nazis thought...were imperfect, or inferior to Aryans."
I can figure out the meaning of "inferior" because I know what "perfect" means, and "im-" often means "not," so I think "inferior" must mean "not perfect."
¶33 "Although the Canadian and British garrison fought bravely..."
I don't know the meaning of "garrison"; it might be a group of soldiers so I'll read on and see if this makes sense.
¶37 "Canadians welcomed the news of Hitler's suicide."
I've never seen the word "suicide" and it seems really important. What did Hitler do? I think I'll ask someone, or look it up.

Encourage students to choose highlighted words and "think aloud" their strategies for figuring out the meanings.

Paraphrasing game

- Print the words and paragraph references used in the previous activity (Let Go of Your Dictionary!) on heavy paper and cut them apart.
- Organize the class into six groups, ensuring that each includes students representing a range of proficiency in English.
- Distribute the word cards evenly among the groups, keeping about five in reserve for exchanges.
- Instruct students to work as a group to find each word in context, rehearse a paraphrase or explanation of the sentence, and be ready to read aloud the sentence and present the paraphrase or explanation.
- Groups may exchange words that are causing difficulty.
- When everyone is ready, start the game. Instruct students to put their words in an envelope. Roll a die to see which group gets a turn. Call on an individual from the group to pull a word from the envelope, direct everyone to find it in the text, read the sentence aloud, and paraphrase or explain it. Coaching by other group members is allowed; this is a co-operative learning activity. If scoring is important to the students, give a point for each paraphrase or explanation that captures the meaning.

Film and read-aloud

Read aloud the case study as students follow in their texts. As a follow-up, you might screen the film, *Enemy Aliens*, which is available from the National Film Board, or read from Shizuye Takashima's *A Child in Prison Camp* (Tundra Books: Montreal, 1974). Excerpts from this book are included in several anthologies.

Class visitors	Invite a speaker or speakers to talk to students about the Holocaust. Make sure that the speakers know that the students are still learning English, and many have had limited exposure to European history. Help students prepare questions beforehand.
Journal responses	Give students a list of some of the feature films about World War II or the Holocaust, from classics to recent works such as *Schindler's List*, that can be rented from video stores. Suggest that they view the videos together at each other's homes. Encourage everyone to watch at least one film and write a personal journal response to it.
Research projects	Students can research many topics, either individually or in groups. Suggested topics can include My Country and World War II, The Blitz in Britain, The Bombing of Pearl Harbor, The War in Asia, The War in Africa, The Holocaust, Military or Political Leaders in World War II, Resistance Movements, The German Occupation, The Bombing of Hiroshima and Nagasaki, and Patriotism and Propaganda.
Reading aloud	Read aloud *Sadako and the Thousand Paper Cranes* by Eleanor Coerr (Putnam's: New York, 1993), a simply written and very moving children's book. If possible, read to small groups so that everyone can see the illustrations in this new edition of the classic story.

Chapter 9: Prosperity and the Cold War: 1945-1963

Features of the Text

This chapter is organized in two main sections: prosperity in the 1950s (cause and effect, description) and the Cold War (sequence, cause and effect). Make sure that students read the chapter introduction. Point out that ¶1 is an advance organizer for the first section (to ¶24) and ¶25 introduces the rest of the chapter. Discuss the figurative meaning of the phrase "sleeping next to an elephant," which is found in ¶25. This expression foreshadows the conflicts described in the rest of the chapter.

A great deal of information is provided in the illustrative material in this chapter. For example, the map on p. 138 illustrates which countries belonged to NATO and which to the Warsaw Pact, and the illustrations on pp. 139-150 provide information about Canadian life in the 1950s. Provide frameworks to help students make oral statements about some of the graphic material. For example, a framework for Figure 9.1 might look like this:

Immigration to Canada increased Immigration to Canada decreased More immigrants arrived Fewer immigrants arrived	between...and... between...and... after during	because... because of... as a result of... in order to...

The reading of some parts of this chapter can be assigned as a jigsaw activity. For example, if the class is divided into groups of four, the section on international crises (¶34-48) can be studied in jigsaw groups, with each student responsible for one of these subtopics: the Korean War; the Suez Crisis; preparing for nuclear war; and the Cuban Missile Crisis.

Prosperity and the Cold War: 1945-1963*
Graphic organizer

This organizer provides an overview of the chapter, showing the main topics and indicating the major points under each. Divide students into six groups and assign each group a different subtopic. Instruct students to skim their own section of the text to find and list the major points. Call on individuals from each group to share with the class so that everyone can complete the organizer before starting to read.

Standard of Living
Pre-reading activity

Introduce and guide a whole-class discussion of this topic by asking questions like:

What is "standard of living"?
What do people need in order to have a high standard of living?

Encourage students to extend their definition of standard of living by going beyond a mere discussion of income levels and material possessions to include public services, such as parks, health care, libraries and educational opportunities, as well as quality-of-life issues, such as freedom from political persecution, low crime rates, etc.

Write the following questions on the chalkboard to guide a small-group discussion. At the end of a specified time, call on individuals to report their group's conclusions.

Do you think that Canada has a high standard of living? Give reasons to support your opinion.
Do you think that it is a government's job to make sure people have a high standard of living?
Why do you think the standard of living in Canada improved after the Second World War?
Do you know of countries in which the standard of living is not the same as Canada's? Give examples.

Prosperity Comes to Canada Again!*
Sentence completion

This task focuses on cause and effect and features this sentence pattern:

The government stimulated investment by creating tax deductions.

    ↑   ↑   ↑   ↑   ↑

  subject   past tense verb   by ...ing   object

Write this example on the chalkboard, label it, and encourage students to follow the pattern.

How Did Prosperity Affect Life in Canada?*
Sentence completion

This activity requires students to complete cause-and-effect statements in response to specific transition words or phrases.

The Life of a Teenager in the 1950s Interview

Invite several teachers who went to school in Canada in the 1950s to visit the class to talk about their experiences as teenagers and high school students. To avoid timetable conflicts, this activity may need to be scheduled outside regular school hours. Ask the teachers to bring yearbooks, scrapbooks, photograph albums, keepsakes, etc. Before the visit, organize students into small groups to brainstorm a list of things they would like to know about (e.g., school, relationships with parents, entertainment, relationships between girls and boys, clothes, jobs, responsibilities, etc.). Each student within a group then chooses a different topic and prepares questions for the visiting teacher. Check the questions for form and content before the visit.

On the day of the visit, assign one teacher to each group. If there are not enough teachers for this, organize a panel; group students according to the topics they have chosen and moderate the interview so that each group has an opportunity to ask several questions.

The Life of a Teenager in the 1950s and Today* Comparison

Group students according to the topics they chose for the previous activity and instruct them to review their information.

Demonstrate how to create a Venn diagram showing similarities and differences: the overlapping area shows features that are common while the separate areas show features that are different. Each group can then create a Venn diagram comparing teen life in the '50s and today on a large sheet of chart paper and post it on the classroom wall.

Distribute the list of phrases for making statements of comparison. Then, invite each group to use information from its Venn diagram to write several statements comparing teen life in the two eras on another sheet of chart paper. Post these and invite students to circulate to read each other's charts and make comments or ask questions.

Journal responses

Invite students to write a journal response on one of the following topics:

Describe the life of a teenager in another country.
Compare school in your home country with school in Canada.
Would you rather live in Canada today or in the 1950s? Why?

How was Canada Involved in World Affairs?* Labelling a map

This activity is designed to follow up a reading of ¶¶26-34. The diagram shows how the world powers were aligned during the Cold War and how Canada related to NATO and the Warsaw Pact. This activity can be re-used in a test.

Canada's Involvement in World Affairs* True or false, paraphrasing

This activity requires students to support their choices by paraphrasing statements from the text.

Governments in the World Today* Class survey, interview

Provide background knowledge and vocabulary before students do this activity (e.g., democracy, dictatorship, one-party system, military regime, totalitarian government, communist, capitalist, free market, nationalized businesses and services, land ownership, etc.).

Before students conduct the interviews, lead a class discussion of how the questions apply to Canada. For example, the government's role in family life in Canada includes protecting women and children from abuse, providing social assistance or tax benefits for families with children, and subsidizing daycare. Encourage students to work together to write a set of questions and check them with you before starting the interviews. Students can report their findings orally or in writing.

How Did Canadians Vote? *
Reading charts

Students combine the information from the sidebar material on pp. 159, 160 and 161 to complete this chart. Make sure they understand the terms "minority government," "majority government" and "opposition."

Chapter 10: French and English Canada after World War II

Features of the Text

Chapter introduction and background	The introduction (in italics, p. 164) summarizes the content of the chapter and ¶¶1-3 provide background information that helps students understand the chapter. Read this material with the students, then assign the pre-reading activity outlined in the Student Activities section to help them review relevant information provided earlier in the text.
Vocabulary	This chapter introduces increasingly abstract concepts and vocabulary such as "heritage," "tension," "terrorism," "separatism," "overthrow," "federalism," "constitution," "referendum," "sovereignty," etc. Many of these words are highlighted in the text. The section on the October Crisis contains a great deal of vocabulary relating to crime.
Present perfect tense	This chapter uses the present perfect tense to describe past events that continue to affect the present. Point out some of the following examples:

Introduction — have influenced
¶2   have come into conflict
¶4   has changed
      have had a major influence
      have made their mark
¶55 still has not signed
      have been disappointed
      have become frustrated
      tension...has increased
      has become a strong political force

Passive verbs	Passive verbs are used frequently in sections of this chapter that focus on events, processes or results rather than on the person(s) responsible. Point out some of the following examples:

¶30 the police were given the right to arrest anybody
¶31 James Cross and his FLQ kidnappers were found
      the kidnappers were flown to Cuba
      members of the FLQ were arrested and charged
      they were sentenced
      436 people were arrested
      20 of them were convicted
¶32 the War Measures Act had never been used

Advance organizers	This chapter includes several paragraphs that function as advance organizers, introducing a major section of text. Point out these paragraphs.

¶4   introduces the content of ¶¶5-27.
¶27 introduces the content of ¶¶28-50.
¶51 introduces the content of the rest of the chapter.

Student Activities

French-English Relations in Canada* Pre-reading activity

This pre-reading organizer helps students activate background knowledge gained from earlier chapters of the text.

Political Conflicts in Canada* Graphic organizer

This organizer focuses on the fundamental beliefs or ideologies of significant Canadian politicians or political groups in the 1950s, 1960s and 1970s. Before distributing the organizer, it's a good idea to create a transparency showing students how to place a name in a particular quadrant on one or both of the diagrams. After reading ¶¶5-32, students can complete the activity either individually or in groups. Then, invite individuals to write labels on the transparency and explain their choices.

What Did They Believe?* Paragraph frames

This writing activity relates to information found in ¶¶5-27.

The October Crisis* Newspaper headlines

To prepare this activity, distribute several different newspapers (e.g., the *Globe and Mail* and a community tabloid) and encourage students to skim the headlines, comparing choice of feature articles, word choice, editorial style and stance, etc. Point out the use of the present tense and the telegraphic style of headlines.

Show students how most news stories are structured: the main points (who, what, when, where, why and how) are outlined in the first few paragraphs and details follow. Explain that this occurs so that editors can cut paragraphs off the bottom of a story to make it fit an available space without losing key information. Help students skim articles to find out who, what, when, where, why and how.

Give each group a set of articles with the headlines cut off and lay the headlines on another table. Invite students to match the headlines with the appropriate articles. Then, distribute the activity.

Students may be interested in talking about "freedom of the press," a concept that may be unfamiliar to those from other countries whose only experience may be with heavily censored or propagandist media.

The October Crisis Roleplay

Divide the class into four groups, each of which will play the role of one of the following:

- Quebec provincial government (Bourassa supporters)
- Front du Libération de Québec (FLQ supporters)
- Parti Québécois (Lévesque supporters)
- Federal government (Trudeau supporters)

Arrange the classroom for discussion and give the following instructions to the groups:

Prepare a statement for your group to make to the other groups, explaining your point of view. Ensure that every student in the group has an opportunity to speak. Your statement should:

— State your group's aims for Quebec's future.
— Identify whether your group is separatist or federalist.
— State your support for or opposition to the use of violence in general.
— State whether your group would support the use of violence at certain times and why.
— Give reasons for your actions in October 1970.
— State your opinion of the actions of other groups, political parties or governments.

Constitutional
Crossfire*
Notemaking

This activity focuses on major conflicts that have surfaced as part of the continuing constitutional debate in Canada. Make a transparency of the chart or draw part of it on the chalkboard and complete one or two boxes, showing students how to summarize a point in one or two words.

Create a
Crossword!*
Crossword puzzles

Organize students into groups of four. Distribute the answers to Crossword Puzzle A to half of the class and the answers to Puzzle B to the other half. Within each group, two students work together to write the Across clues while the other two write the Down clues. The clues should be based on the content of the chapter and include a paragraph reference. Students can use the puzzles from Chapters 3 and 7 as models.

After checking their clues with each other and you, members of each group prepare a final version of their puzzle that includes the blank grid and both sets of clues. Each "A" group then exchanges puzzles with one of the "B" groups. Students can solve the puzzles in groups or in pairs.

Cultural profiles

Read aloud the case study about Italians in Canada and the profile of Johnny Lombardi. Suggest that students use one of these as a model for writing an account either of the arrival and progress in Canada of people from their own cultural group or of a prominent individual in their community. Encourage them to illustrate their work with photographs and drawings and create a class display of their writing.

Aspects of
My Culture*
Oral presentations

This can be a group or individual assignment. The presentations may be made to the whole class or smaller groups. During the planning stage, discuss evaluation criteria and invite students to help create an evaluation sheet that they can use both to help plan their own work and to evaluate each other's presentations.

Journal responses   Invite students to write journal responses on one of the following topics:

Are there times when violence is a good way to resolve conflict? Use your personal experience to explain your opinion.

What rights do you have? Should you have more rights than you do? Think about your rights as a member of your family, as a high school student, as a male or female, and as a member of a cultural or linguistic group.

Chapter 11: Canada's Economy and Culture since 1945

Features of the Text

Text organization

You can help students become more independent readers of academic text by emphasizing how text is organized. A knowledge of text organization is very helpful when students are skimming to find main ideas or searching for details and examples.

- Like previous chapters, Chapter 11 has an introduction (in italics, p. 186) that serves as an advance organizer for the whole chapter.
- The pre-reading question at the beginning of each major section of text serves as an advance organizer for the section. These questions are also listed in the chapter contents at the beginning of the book.
- The first paragraph of each major section provides more detail about the content of the section.
- The first sentence of each paragraph is usually the topic sentence, a general statement about the details included in the rest of the paragraph.
- The sidebar material, illustrations and case studies often illustrate or elaborate on a specific point that may have been mentioned only briefly in the main body of the text.

Vocabulary

In this chapter, students will encounter new vocabulary related to economics and culture. New vocabulary is no longer highlighted in the text. By now, students should be applying the strategies outlined in the flow chart titled "Let Go of Your Dictionary!" that was introduced in Chapter 8. Review this with students.

Student Activities

Canada's Economy and Culture since 1945*
Graphic organizer

This organizer provides a graphic framework only. As a pre-reading activity, invite students to survey the table of contents for the chapter, as well as the chapter itself, and fill in the appropriate topics and subtopics. Then, as they read each section, they can fill in the main points. Remind them that the question at the beginning of each section is a guide to the main idea of the section.

A completed organizer is provided. Before students begin, show part of it to them as an example or invite them to check their work against it as they complete each section. While the students' wording will vary from the model, the content should be similar.

A Delicate Balance*
Decision-making

Invite students to refer to the text, ¶¶4-17, to find the advantages and disadvantages of American investment in Canada, then list these on the appropriate side of the scale. Then ask them whether, in their opinion, the advantages outweigh the disadvantages or vice versa. Students can discuss this question in groups, but don't push them to reach consensus; it's more important for them to develop—and support—an opinion. Point out that it is not the number of advantages or disadvantages that should be considered, but their relative weight. It is possible that someone may consider a specific advantage or disadvantage so significant that it outweighs all other considerations.

I Recommend...* *Letter-writing*	This activity provides practice in developing paragraphs and raises the students' awareness of their democratic rights in Canada.
Free Trade: A Century of Controversy* *Finding details*	Instruct students to refer to the text, ¶¶18-31, to find the details and examples needed to fill in the chart.
Not a Leg to Stand On* *Recognizing opinion*	Invite students to refer to the cartoon on p. 191 and the text in ¶¶33-41 to complete this matching exercise.
What Is Canadian Culture?* *Graphic organizer*	Filling in this organizer encourages students to examine aspects of Canadian culture described in ¶¶43-47 and in some of the visual material.
Why and How Canada Promotes Canadian Culture* *Matching activity*	As students return to the text to complete this matching activity, their awareness of Canadian culture will increase.
Who Influences Us?* *Class survey*	Completing this survey will help develop students' awareness of the cultural influences that affect people living in Canada. Use this opportunity to explain the difference between primary research, which they are about to do, and secondary research, which relies on other sources. Instruct each student to interview 10 other students. If yours is an ESL class, try teaming up with a "mainstream" class that has a more representative sample of the student population. To find trends or patterns and write their conclusions, students combine their results, either in groups or as a class.
Canada's Economy and Culture* *Cloze*	Students may need to practise pronouncing the words on the first page (see p. 10 of the introduction to this resource book). Help them recognize where the main stress falls in each word and point out shifts in stress (e.g., 'benefit—bene'ficial). Students can complete the assignment for homework or as a group activity. When you take it up, call on individual students to read a passage aloud to the class.
Journal responses	Invite students to write a personal response to one of the following questions: Do you feel that your own culture is valued in your school? Give reasons for your opinion. Would you like your school to have a more multicultural curriculum? Give reasons for your opinion.

Chapter 12: Being or Becoming a Canadian

Features of the Text

Content

This chapter is one of the most important in the textbook, especially for students from other countries. It contains essential information about how Canadian government works and explains democratic rights that may not exist in some students' home countries.

Note: It is not necessary to cover this chapter last. For example, if an election should take place during the school year, you may choose to introduce this material at that time.

Organization

Remind students of the features of text organization outlined in the resource material for Chapter 11.

Vocabulary

In this chapter, students will encounter new vocabulary related to law and government. As in the previous chapter, new vocabulary is not highlighted. At this stage, students should be applying the strategies for decoding meaning outlined in Chapter 8.

Additional resources

A variety of resources that supplement the material in this chapter is available free-of-charge or at nominal cost.

- Contact the provincial ministry responsible for resettlement services and citizenship to check the availability of resource material for newcomers to Canada.

The following resources are available from the federal government.

Bell, Jill & Marjatta Holt. *It's Your Right*. Ottawa: Minister of Supply and Services Canada, 1988.

This kit includes an illustrated, simply written student's manual covering the following topics: basic rights and freedoms; tenants' rights; age; disability; sexual harassment; equal pay; employment rights; and race, colour and ethnic origin. It can be ordered from the Human Rights Directorate, Department of the Secretary of State of Canada, Ottawa, Ont. K1A OM5.

Citizenship and Immigration Canada. *Canada: A Source Book for Orientation, Language and Settlement Workers*. Ottawa: Minister of Supply and Services Canada.

This resource binder for teachers includes reproducible material for students. Order from Citizenship and Immigration Canada, Settlement Branch, Phase II, 5th Floor, 140 Promenade de Portage, Hull, Que. K1A 1L1.

Citizenship and Immigration Canada. *A Newcomer's Introduction to Canada*. Ottawa: Minister of Supply and Services Canada.

This very simply written student material accompanies *Canada: A Source Book for Orientation, Language and Settlement Workers*. The chapter titled "Your Rights and Obligations" provides a simple introduction to topics covered in more depth in Chapter 12 of *My Country, Our History*.

Student Activities

Using the visual material

Before starting the chapter, use the illustration on p. 201 to introduce a pre-reading activity. Invite students to work in groups to brainstorm answers to the following questions about each photograph:

Who or what is in the photograph?
What is happening?
What is this photograph about?
What role of government is shown in the photograph?

Applying for Canadian Citizenship* Interview, filling in a form

Free support material on citizenship is available from the Department of the Secretary of State of Canada, Ottawa, Ontario K1A OM5. Every province also has a ministry or department responsible for resettlement and citizenship.

Rights and Responsibilities of Canadian Citizenship* Graphic organizer

Invite students to complete this organizer as they read ¶¶5-16. If groups of four are divided into two sets of partners, one pair can be assigned to fill in the material on rights while the other fills in the material on responsibilities. Once they've finished, instruct students to close their texts and explain what they've found out to the other pair. Encourage students to make statements about the rights of Canadians in comparison with the rights of citizens of other countries.

Protect Your Rights!* Roleplay or graphic arts

Depending on their aptitudes and interests, students may choose to complete either the roleplay or the cartoon activity. For the roleplay assignment, organize students into groups of five. They may complete the cartoon story individually or with a partner. The roleplays can be presented to the class and the cartoon stories can be displayed in class.

Follow up by introducing a class discussion on this topic: If you were a Human Rights Commission officer, what would you do to resolve these conflicts? Why?

Business letter or memo

Show students models of formal business letters and memoranda to help them complete one of the following writing assignments:

- As the Human Rights Commission officer, write a letter either to the personnel officer and manager of the company that refused to hire Tru or to the manager of the department store.
- As the manager or personnel officer, answer the letter from the Human Rights Commission officer.
- As the Human Rights Commission officer, write a memo to your manager explaining the problem and recommending a course of action to resolve the problem.

*How to Find a Government Service** *Using the Blue Pages*	Prepare for this activity, which introduces the Blue Pages and helps students distinguish among the levels of government and the services they provide, by referring students to the photographs and sidebar question on p. 214.
*How to Use the Blue Pages** *Identifying key terms**	For this activity, you will need enough telephone books for students to share with a partner. Students can complete the assignment for homework and compare their results in class the next day.
*What Services Do Governments Provide?** *Survey*	This makes an excellent small-group activity. You may suggest that students collate the results to create a class chart. To complete this task, students need to use the following patterns for asking questions:

Does the government of _____ provide...?
Does the _____ government provide...?
Does the government provide _____ in _____?
What services does the government provide in _____?

*Who's Who in Canadian Government?** *Reading for details*	Instruct students to refer to ¶¶24-37 to complete this chart.
*Elections in Canada** *Cloze*	This activity helps students review major concepts and internalize important vocabulary found in ¶¶58-65.
*Becoming a Canadian Citizen** *Roleplay*	This activity can be used to review important concepts presented in this chapter. Invite each student to write 10 questions, then check the content and grammar with you. Organize students in pairs to interview each other.
Journal responses	Suggest that students write journal responses on one of the following topics:

Why I am glad I live in Canada.
Why I will (will not) become a citizen of Canada.
What citizenship means to me.
A students' rights code.

Case study	Read aloud the case study on p. 220 and encourage students to comment on the various reasons people choose to leave their homeland and come to Canada.
	Invite students to interview each other about their own experiences, using indirect questions (see Children at Work, Chapter 5). Write these patterns on the chalkboard as question starters:

Please tell me when _____ to Canada.
I'd like to know why _____ to Canada.

I'm interested in whether _____ any strong memories about your country.

I wonder if _____ a special place or person that you miss in your country?

Tell me how _____ about being in Canada now.

I'd like to know what _____ in the future.

Suggest that students write profiles of each other based on the interview. Take photographs of all the students and collate the profiles into a class booklet. Make copies for students to take home at the end of the course.

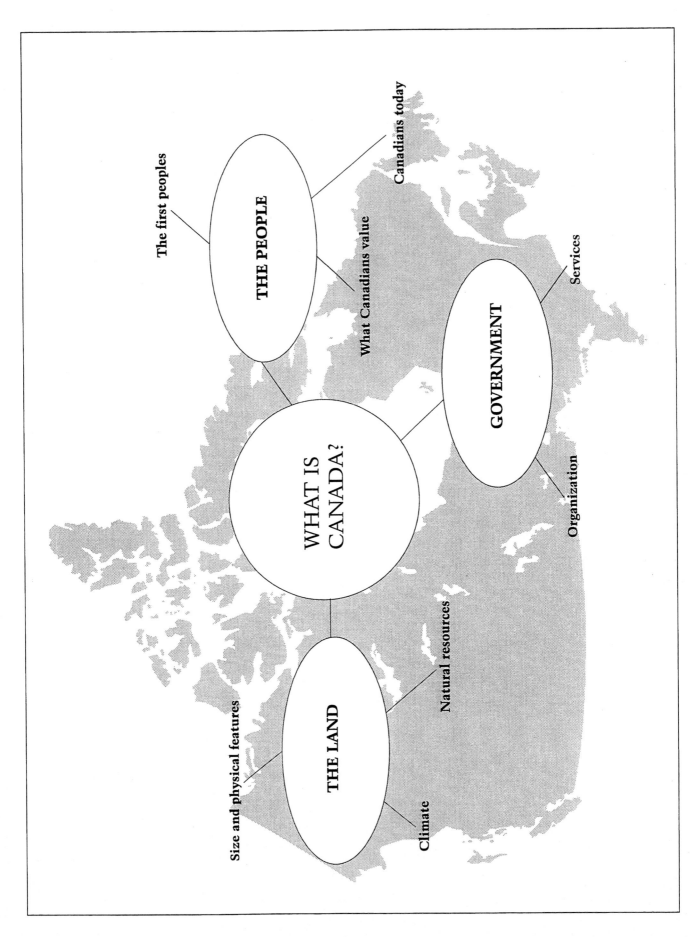

WHAT IS CANADA?

THE PEOPLE
The first peoples
Canadians today
What Canadians value

GOVERNMENT
Services
Organization

THE LAND
Size and physical features
Natural resources
Climate

LET GO OF YOUR DICTIONARY!

Using the rest of a sentence or paragraph to infer the meaning of new words

What do you think "infer" means?
Sometimes it is better to infer the meaning of new words than to stop and look them up in the dictionary. The dictionary can slow you down and it doesn't always give the exact meaning the writer intended. Very often, you can correctly guess what a word means by looking at the rest of the sentence or paragraph.

Find the words in the text that have the following meanings:

¶ 1	the people who live there	_____
¶ 4	things that people want to sell	_____
¶ 7	the land in the North, where trees don't grow	_____
¶ 8	gold, copper, and other metals	_____
¶ 9	in the country; outside the cities	_____
¶ 10	in towns and cities	_____
¶ 14	the money that people receive	_____
¶ 15	for the whole country	_____
¶ 21	two kinds of animal	_____
		_____
¶ 22	way of life	_____
¶ 23	speaking many languages	_____
¶ 25	the names of two diseases	_____
		_____
¶ 25	people who study history	_____
¶ 26	the people who lived before us	_____
¶ 27	people who came to live here	_____
	people who supported Britain	_____
¶ 28	100 years	_____

SIMILAR OR DIFFERENT?

Comparing Canada with another country

Complete this chart with information about Canada and one other country.

Country	Canada	
Climate	*temperate; colder in the North*	
Oceans	*Arctic* *Pacific*	
Lakes and rivers	*Great Lakes*	
Mountains		
Islands	*Vancouver Island*	
Resources and products		

Use the information from the completed chart to write some sentences about the similarities and differences between the countries. Use some of these expressions:

Similarities	Examples
Canada and _____ both have (produce). . .	Canada and China **both** produce wheat.
Canada and _____ are both . . .	Canada and China are **both** large countries.
Both Canada and _____ have (are) (produce) . . .	**Both** Canada and China produce steel.
. . ., and Canada does (is) too.	Poland produces steel, and Canada **does, too.**
. . ., and so does (is) Canada.	Poland produces steel, **and so does** Canada.
. . . and neither does (is) Canada.	Poland doesn't produce bananas, **and neither does** Canada.
Neither Canada nor _____ is (has) (produces). . .	**Neither** Canada **nor** Poland produces bananas.
Differences	**Examples**
. . . bigger (smaller) (fewer) (more) (warmer) (less) than . . .	Jamaica is much **smaller than** Canada.
. . . not as big (small) (many) (much) as . . .	Canada is **not as big as** Russia.
. . ., but . . . doesn't (isn't).	Canada has a lot of lakes and rivers, **but** Somalia doesn't.
. . ., whereas Canada is (has) (produces). . .	India produces a lot of rice, **whereas** Canada produces a lot of wheat.

FACTS ABOUT CANADA

Choose words to complete each paragraph:

located   population   surrounded   urban   temperate   rural

Most Canadians live in _____ areas, and about 30 per cent of the Canadian _____ lives in the big cities of Toronto, Vancouver and Montreal. These cities are _____ in the southern part of Canada, where the climate is _____.

resources   products   service   produce   depend   manufacturing

Many jobs in Canada _____ on natural _____ such as trees, fish and oil. In the cities, many people work in the _____ industries, making _____ in factories. _____ industries such as finance, communications and government are also important in urban areas.

cultures   resources   historians   First Nations   settlers   ancestors

Canada's _____ were the first people to live in Canada. Their _____ were here thousands of years before the first Europeans arrived. They believed that the land and the natural _____ belonged to everyone, but the European _____ wanted to own the land.

century   colony   relationship   symbol   ancestors   multicultural

Canada is one of the most _____ countries in the world. Canadians with _____ from many different parts of the world live here. For about two hundred years, Canada was a British _____, and we still have a very close _____ with Britain. For example, the Queen of England is a very important _____ of government in Canada.

SUFFIXES THAT MEAN "SOMEONE WHO. . ."

Look at the endings of these words from Chapter 1. These endings mean a person. For example, a *farmer* is someone who owns or works on a farm; an *ancestor* is someone in the same family or cultural group who lived a long time ago; *descendants* are people who came from the ancestors; an *activist* is someone who is active for or against an idea or system; a *Canadian* is someone who lives in Canada.

Word endings are called suffixes. These suffixes mean "someone who. . ."

-er	**-or**	**-ant**	**-ist**	**-ian, -an**
miner	ancestor	immigrant	Loyalist	Canadian
farmer		descendant	activist	European
hunter				historian
settler				American
teacher				African
lawyer				

Write five sentences, using a word from each of the lists above.

A _____ is someone who _____

A _____ is someone who _____

A _____ is someone who _____

A _____ is someone who _____

A _____ is someone who _____

Now write some sentences about other words you know that have the same suffixes.

A _____ is someone who _____

A _____ is someone who _____

A _____ is someone who _____

A _____ is someone who _____

A _____ is someone who _____

CANADA: FACTS AND FIGURES

Choose words and expressions from this list to complete the sentences about the graphs and charts in Chapter 1.

twice as much as
half as many as
fourth highest
times as many as
three times more than
third largest
__ per cent higher than

twice as many as
second highest
three times as high as
three times higher than
a quarter the size of
fourth largest
__ per cent more than

half as much as
third highest
three times as big as
three times larger than
second largest
__ per cent lower than
__ per cent fewer than

Figure 1.1, page 8

The United States is the _____ country in the world.

Sudan is about _____ Canada.

Figure 1.2, page 8

Canada has about _____ people _____ Nigeria.

India has the _____ population in the world.

Table 1.1, page 13

The average income in Newfoundland is about _____ the national average.

The average income in Yukon is about _____ the average income in Prince Edward Island.

Figure 1.6, page 19

The number of immigrants from Hong Kong was almost _____ the number of immigrants from Great Britain in 1991.

Page 19

There are almost _____ English speakers _____ French speakers in Canada.

There are about _____ German speakers _____ Punjabi speakers in Canada.

CANADA'S FIRST NATIONS: CONTACT

How did the arrival of Europeans change the lives of the people of Canada's First Nations?

Many of the first Europeans who arrived in Canada traded with First Nations groups for animal furs. Because the fur trade was very profitable, the Europeans started permanent settlements here and the European population increased. The fur trade changed the relationship between First Nations peoples and the animals they hunted. Before the Europeans arrived, First Nations groups hunted only what they needed. This meant that there were always enough animals to meet their needs and that they didn't have to travel far to find them. They respected the animals they hunted because they depended on them for their lives.

After European fur traders introduced guns and the idea of killing animals to make money, the number of animals decreased. As a result, hunting became harder and the First Nations peoples began to depend on European products. Because finding animals was harder, First Nations hunters had to travel farther from their own communities, sometimes to areas used by other First Nations groups. This caused wars between groups.

As more and more Europeans arrived, they pushed First Nations groups out of their traditional territories. Often, they had to move to areas where food was scarce. As a result, their health suffered. In addition, the settlers brought diseases, such as smallpox and tuberculosis, that were new in Canada. These diseases destroyed many Native communities.

The settlers also wanted First Nations peoples to obey European laws, live, dress and think like Europeans, and worship a European God. It was not easy for First Nations peoples to change their beliefs and way of life. They often suffered great hardship and conflict.

Find some changes in the way First Nations people lived. Find the cause of each of these changes and complete this chart.

Cause	Effect
Europeans introduced guns.	*The number of animals decreased.*

THE STORY OF HARRIET TUBMAN

Harriet Tubman was born in the United States, but her story is part of the history of Canada, too.

Harriet was born a slave in the southern United States, where African slaves did most of the work. Until 1834, there were slaves in Canada too. Slaves were not free; they did not even own themselves. Their owners could beat them and punish them, or sell them to other slaveowners. Harriet's owner sold her two sisters, and she never saw them again. Harriet began to dream of freedom.

As a young woman, Harriet heard many stories about the "Underground Railroad." This wasn't a real railroad, and it wasn't under the ground either. "Underground" means "secret" and the "railroad" was a secret way out of the southern United States to freedom in the North. Many people, white and black, secretly helped the refugee slaves escape; they were called "station-masters" and "conductors" and they hid the refugees in "safe houses."

SLAVE AUCTION AT RICHMOND, VIRGINIA

In 1849, Harriet took the Underground Railroad and escaped to the North. After about a year of freedom, she secretly began to travel back to the South to rescue other people, including members of her own family. This was very dangerous for Harriet, but she believed that freedom was more important than personal danger. She was very brave.

In 1850, it became even harder to escape from slavery. A new law in the United States said that anyone who escaped to the North was still the property of the owner; the owner could hire people to capture the "property" and enslave them again. So the Underground Railroad had to take people all the way to Canada. Harriet and her family moved to St. Catharines in Ontario, but Harriet continued to work as a conductor. She led hundreds of people out of slavery. People began to call her "Moses," after Moses who led the Jews out of slavery in Egypt. At one time, there was a reward of $40,000 for anyone who captured her, dead or alive. But nobody ever caught her.

When slavery ended in the United States, Harriet Tubman returned; but many African American families stayed in Canada, where they helped develop the new land. Canadians and Americans remember Harriet Tubman and the Underground Railroad as symbols of freedom and bravery.

True or false?

Refer to the story to find your evidence!

Harriet Tubman was a famous Canadian. *This is true (false) because* <u>she was born in the United States.</u>

There were never any slaves in Canada. *This is true/false because* _____
_____

Some white people in the United States did not agree with slavery. *This is true/false because* _____
_____

Harriet Tubman was a big problem for the slaveowners. *This is true/false because*
_____

African Canadians have a long history in Canada. *This is true/false because* __
_____

Choose the words

Look at these words in the story, then choose the correct word to complete the sentences:

brave, bravery; free, freedom; South, southern; slave, slavery, enslave; danger, dangerous

The Underground Railroad brought many African Americans to _____ in Ontario.

_____ ended in Canada in 1834.

_____ was the most important thing in life to Harriet Tubman.

Being a conductor on the Underground railroad was very _____ work.

Many _____ people worked on the Underground Railroad.

WHAT DO WE KNOW ABOUT COLONIZATION?

1. Discuss these questions in your group.

Do you know which European countries used to own colonies in North and South America? Make a list.

What other countries do you know that are or used to be colonies of a European country? Make a list

2. Make a chart.

In this class, who was born in a country that used to be a colony of another country? In this class, who was born in a country that owns or used to own colonies? Interview everyone in your group and record the information on a chart like the one shown below.

Now collect information from the other groups in the class and complete the chart. Group people from the same country together.

Name(s) of students					
Country of origin					
Is a colony of. . .					
Used to be a colony of ...					
Has always been independent (✔)					
Owns or used to own colonies (✔)					

3. Finish these statements about the chart.

____ per cent of the students in this class come from countries that own or used to own colonies.

About ____ per cent of us come from countries that are or used to be colonies of other countries.

____ per cent of us come from countries that have neither been colonies nor owned any.

CANADA BECOMES A COUNTRY

Early Canada: Description

There were colonies belonging to _____ and _____

A change: Event→result

Event

There was a war between _____ and _____

→

Result

Life in British North America: Description

People

Way of Life

A change: Problems→ solutions

Problem:

People were worried about:

1. *Political problems.*

2. *The economy: they might not be able to. . .*

3. *Defence: they were afraid of. . .*

4. *The cost of. . .*

–¿→

Solutions

Most people thought that Confederation would:

1.

2.

3.

4.

Resolution and description

Therefore, in 1867. . . .

The new Dominion of Canada consisted of four provinces.

There were two levels of government: the _____ government and the _____ government..

MORE SUFFIXES THAT MEAN "SOMEONE WHO"

In Chapter 1, we looked at some words with suffixes meaning "someone who...."
In Chapter 2, you will find more words that use these suffixes.

1. *Refer to ¶¶ 7, 8, 9 and 13. Find the words with the following suffixes and list them here.*

-er	-or	-ant	-ist	-ian,-an
_____	_____	_____	_____	_____
_____	_____	_____	_____	_____
_____	_____			

2. *Write five sentences, using a word from each of the lists.*

A _____ *is someone who* _____

A _____ *is someone who* _____

A _____ *is someone who* _____

A _____ *is someone who* _____

A _____ *is someone who* _____

3. Some words don't follow this pattern (see ¶9).

A *smith* is someone who makes things from metal; e.g., a *tinsmith* makes cooking pots out of tin.

The suffix -*man* was once very common, but today many people prefer to use "gender-neutral" words; e.g., *fisher* instead of *fisherman, craftsperson* instead of *craftsman, businesspeople* instead of *businessmen,* etc. A *lumberjack* works in the forest cutting down trees, but Jack is a man's name. Can we use another word that includes women?

Question: Do words for people's job in other languages show whether the person is male or female?

Ask some other students about their languages and fill in the following chart.

Language	Do the words for people's jobs show whether the person is male or female?	Examples
English	Some words do, but they are changing.	"Salesman" and "saleswoman" have changed to "salesperson" or "sales clerk."
French	Most words show whether the person is male or female.	2 words for "director": "directeur" (m), "directrice" (f).

THE AFFIX SYSTEM

If you understand the "affix system" of English, you can figure out the meanings of many words you have never seen before! Here is how it works: many English words consist of a **base word** and **affixes**. For example, in the word *farmer*, *farm* is the base word and *-er* is an affix.

AFFIXES
An affix is a small part of a word that we can add or fix to the beginning or end of a word.

PREFIXES
Prefixes are at the beginning of a word. For example: **a**ffix, **suf**fix, **pre**fix. **Prefixes change the meaning of the word.** For example:

Prefix	Usual Meaning	Example
a-/af-	on	affix
cent-	hundred	century
con-	with, together	Confederation
de-	from, down, away	defend
dis-	not	disagree
im-	not	impossible
in-	not	independent
manu-	by hand	manufacture
multi-	many	multicultural
pre-	before	prefix
sub-/suf-	under, close to	suffix
un-	not	unhappy
uni-	one	unite, union

SUFFIXES
Suffixes are at the end of a word. For example: govern**ment**, govern**or**. **Suffixes usually give grammatical information.** For example:

Suffix	Usual Meaning	Example
-ant	noun: a person	immigrant
-er	noun: a person	hunter
-ian/-an	noun: a person	historian
-ist	noun: a person	loyalist
-or	noun: a person	governor
-ence	abstract noun	independence
-ion	abstract noun	union
-ment	abstract noun	government
-tion	abstract noun	Confederation
-ry/-y	abstract noun	slavery
-ate	verb	immigrate
-ize	verb	symbolize
-al	adjective	federal
-ic	adjective	economic
-ent	adjective	independent
-ful	adjective	resourceful
-ed	past tense	depended
-s	plural	resources

A "word family" is a group of words that are related to each other. Here are the families of some of the words you have read in Chapters 1 and 2:

Common nouns	Abstract nouns	Verbs	Adjectives
dependant	dependence independence	depend	dependent independent
	agreement disagreement	agree disagree	agreeable disagreeable
colonist	colony	colonize	colonial
loyalist	loyalty		loyal
naturalist	nature		natural unnatural
	culture	cultivate	cultural multicultural
migrant immigrant emigrant	migration immigration emigration	migrate immigrate emigrate	migrant immigrant emigrant
symbol	symbolism	symbolize	symbolic
governor	government	govern	governmental
	federation Confederation	federate	federal
	province		provincial
politician	politics	politicize politick	politicized political
historian	history		historical
	resource		resourceful
product	production	produce	productive
descendant	descent	descend	descended
slave	slavery	enslave	enslaved
	freedom	free	free
co-operator	co-operation	co-operate	co-operative
defendant	defence	defend	defensive

Choose words from the families to complete these sentences. You may need to add -ed or -s at the end of some of the words.

Canada's First Nations are the _____ of the first people in Canada. Some _____ believe that the first people came here from Asia many thousands of years ago.

Britain and France _____ North America during the 1500s.

In the American colonies, many of the _____ wanted to be _____ of Britain. They fought a war against Britain; this was called the American War of _____. The American colonists who wanted to stay _____ to Britain came to live in Canada.

Life for the first European _____ was very hard. They did not have much, but they were very _____ and worked in _____ together.

Many African Americans escaped from _____ in the United States and came to live in Canada.

During the last 500 years, people from all over the world have _____ to Canada. Today, Canada is one of the most _____ countries in the world.

There is still _____ between French-speaking and English-speaking Canadians. Today, one of Canada's biggest _____ questions is how to keep the country together.

The _____ government makes decisions for the nation, but the _____ governments look after health and education.

Today, the maple leaf _____ Canada.

JIGSAW WORD PUZZLE: A

Work with your group to complete this puzzle and find the hidden word!

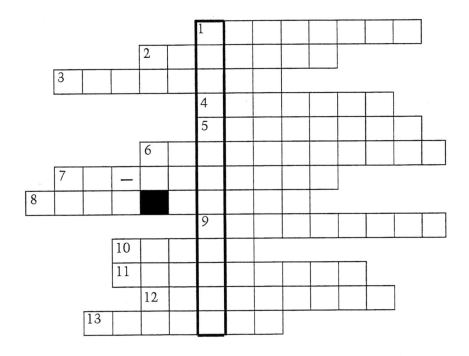

1. Begins with C.
2. It's a noun.
3. Very important.
4. Has an adjective suffix.
5. Has an adjective suffix.
6. Begins with a prefix that means "not."
7. You usually get better results if you do this.
8. Between Canada and the United States.
9. Chapter 2 is all about this.
10. Get together!
11. This word is about power.
12. There were four of these.
13. Has a prefix that means "away."

The hidden word is _____. It means _____.

JIGSAW WORD PUZZLE: B

Work with your group to complete this puzzle and find the hidden word!

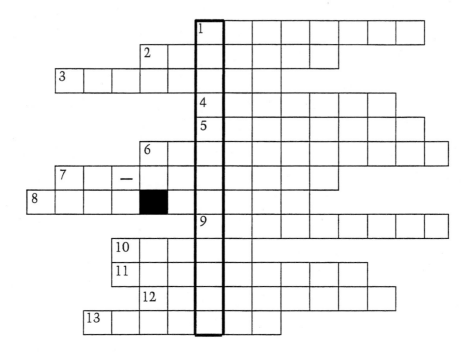

1. There were 7 in British North America.
2. You can sell this.
3. Begins with G.
4. About government.
5. It's about $$$$.
6. Has an adjective suffix of 3 letters.
7. You have to do this to complete this puzzle.
8. Without taxes.
9. Ends with T.
10. Work together.
11. Ends with an adjective suffix.
12. One of them is a small island.
13. Begins with D.

The hidden word is _____. It means _____.

JIGSAW WORD PUZZLE: C

Work with your group to complete this puzzle and find the hidden word!

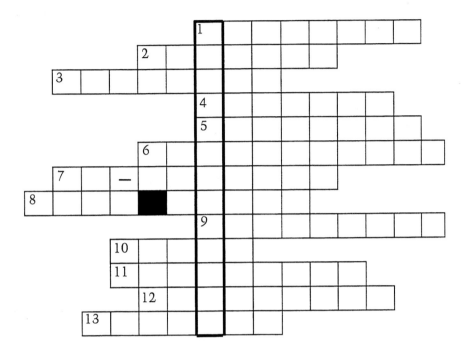

1. Plural noun.
2. It's a word in chemistry.
3. Has a suffix meaning "someone who ..."
4. Not provincial.
5. Has a suffix of two letters.
6. Strong.
7. Ends with a verb suffix.
8. We have this now.
9. Begins with A.
10. Join together!
11. In Canada, language is a _____ question.
12. Now there are 10.
13. The work of the army.

The hidden word is _____. It means _____.

JIGSAW WORD PUZZLE: D

Work with your group to complete this puzzle and find the hidden word!

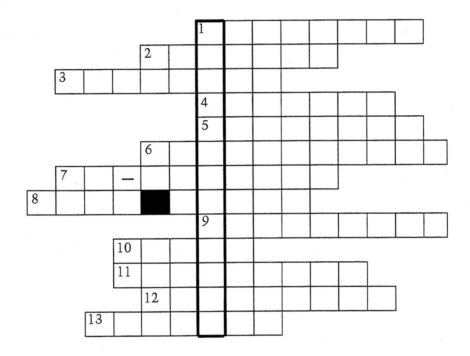

1. They were not independent.
2. It's a word in mathematics.
3. Not the Queen.
4. A big word in Ottawa.
5. Does not end in *-al*.
6. Doesn't need help.
7. Rhymes with "immigrate."
8. Buying and selling.
9. Has a noun suffix of 4 letters.
10. Come together.
11. Begins with P.
12. Plural noun.
13. Ends with E.

The hidden word is _____. It means _____.

WISHES, HOPES, PLANS, FEARS AND WORRIES

*Complete the sentences to show how either the colonists or the British government felt about the future, or what they thought **would happen** or **might happen** in the future. The information is in ¶¶14-18.*

Choose from these expressions to describe how they felt or what they thought:

was (were) afraid that...	was (were) worried that...	hoped that...
thought that...	believed that...	did not believe that...
doubted that...	was (were) (not) sure that...	was (were) (not) convinced that....

Here's an example:
*The colonists **were afraid that** that if the United States ended the free trade agreement, **they would not be able to sell their goods in the United States.***

*Farmers and businesspeople **believed** that **they might lose business if the free trade agreement ended.***

Some farmers and businesspeople _____ *that Confederation was a good idea because* _____ .

Some politicians _____ *that Confederation* _____

_____

Some colonists _____ *that Confederation* _____

_____ *to defend*

themselves against the United States.

Some people did not support the idea of Confederation; they _____

that _____ .

The British government _____ *that Confederation would be a good idea because* _____ .

THE FATHERS OF CONFEDERATION

A Research Assignment

This is a completed outline for a research assignment on John A. Macdonald.

Name: John A. Macdonald

Dates: 1815-1891

Country of Origin: Scotland

Place of Birth: Glasgow, Scotland

Education: Left school at age 15 to start training as a lawyer

Languages: English

Occupation:
• Lawyer
• Canada West leader
• Prime Minister of Canada

Hopes, wishes, plans, interests:
• Wanted to develop Canada.
• Wanted to develop railways in Canada.
• Wanted more immigrants to come to Canada.
• Wanted more settlers to come to Western Canada.

Achievements:
• He was a "Father of Confederation."
• He became Canada's first prime minister.
• The Queen of England knighted him: he became **Sir** John A. Macdonald

Other interesting information:
John A. Macdonald drank a lot!

THE FATHERS OF CONFEDERATION

A Research Assignment

Complete this outline by filling in the missing information.

Name: _____ Cartier

Dates: _____

Place of Birth: St. Antoine

Country of Origin: British North American Colony: _____

Education: _____

Languages: French and English

Occupation:
• _____
• Canada East leader

Hopes, wishes, plans, interests:
• Wanted Quebec to be able to keep French culture and _____
_____ at the same time.

• Wanted to encourage British Columbia and Manitoba to _____

Achievements:
• A leading railway lawyer and businessperson in Montreal.
• The Queen of England knighted him: he became _____

• _____

Other interesting information:

THE FATHERS OF CONFEDERATION

A Research Assignment

Complete this outline by filling in the missing information.

Name: George Brown

Dates: _____

Place of Birth: _____

Country of Origin: Scotland

Education: _____

Languages: French and English

Occupation:
• _____
• Canada West leader

Hopes, wishes, plans, interests:
• He enjoyed newspaper reporting.
• He supported Confederation.
• He disliked John A. Macdonald.

Achievements:
• He started a newspaper called _____. This is
  now Canada's national newspaper, called _____.
• He was the first political leader to suggest _____ as a solution
  to Canada's problems.
• He was a "Father of Confederation."

Other interesting information:

QUEEN VICTORIA

A Research Assignment

Complete this outline by filling in the missing information.

Name: Queen Victoria

Dates: _____

Place of Birth: _____

Country of Origin: Britain

Education: _____

Languages: _____

Occupation:
- Queen of England, Wales, Scotland and Ireland
- Queen of Canada
- Empress of _____

Hopes, wishes, plans, interests:
- _____
- _____
- She had a strong sense of duty.

Achievements:
- She ruled as Queen for _____ years.
- She chose the city of Ottawa to be Canada's capital.
- Many places and streets all over Canada have her name: for example, _____, _____, and _____.
- Canada's holiday on _____ is Victoria Day.

Other interesting information:

DECISIONS, DECISIONS . . .

SHOULD WE JOIN CONFEDERATION?

	ADVANTAGES?	DISADVANTAGES?	Yes or No?
Nova Scotia ¶¶2,3			
The Métis in Rupert's Land ¶¶6-10			
British Columbia ¶¶12, 13			
Prince Edward Island ¶14			
First Nations ¶¶15-19			

EXPANSION OF THE COUNTRY

True or False?

Refer to the text to find your evidence!

Not everyone was happy with the idea of Confederation. (¶¶1-3)

I think this is true (false) because _____

_____

The plans for expansion did not go smoothly. (¶¶6-9)

I think this is true (false) because _____

_____

The Métis got what they wanted. (¶¶10-11)

I think this is true (false) because _____

_____

Canada's First Nations gave up their land by choice. (¶¶15-19)

I think this is true (false) because _____

_____

Most Canadians supported Macdonald's National Policy. (¶23)

I think this is true (false) because _____

_____

The government built the railway. (¶¶25-26)

I think this is true (false) because _____

_____

Macdonald's National Policy was a complete success. (¶¶24-29)

I think this is true (false) because _____

_____

CONFLICTS AND SOLUTIONS

Main Ideas and Examples

In this chapter, you read about some solutions to conflicts. Some of these solutions were successful, some were not successful.

Refer to the chapter to find examples of different kinds of solutions.

Main ideas about solutions to conflict	Examples
A solution is not successful if it does not satisfy most of the people involved.	¶¶6-9
A solution is successful when it satisfies most of the people involved.	¶¶10-11
A solution is successful when both sides feel that it is fair.	¶¶12,13
A solution is not successful when one side feels that it is unfair.	p. 38: Piapot and Sweetgrass

MORE AFFIXES!

You have learned how the affix system works in English. Here are some more affixes that it helps to know, with examples from Chapter 3.

PREFIXES

Prefix	Usual Meaning	Example
bi-	two	bilingual
pro-	forward, in front	progress
		prosperity
		produce
		protect
ex-	out	expand
		execute
trans-	across	transfer
hect-	hundred	hectare

SUFFIXES

Suffix	Usual Meaning	Example
-sion	noun	expansion
-ity	noun	prosperity
-age	noun	advantage
-ous	adjective	advantageous
-ed	adjective	experienced
		satisfied
		worried
		prejudiced
		mounted
-ese	adjective	Chinese
-ite	adjective or noun	Mennonite
-en	verb	threaten
		strengthen
-ure	noun	culture

Using your knowledge of the affix system, choose the best word from the words in brackets to complete these sentences.

Confederation _____ the colonies into a country.
(union, unite, united, unity)

After Confederation, Canada had a lot more _____.
(depend, dependent, independent, independence)

Howe believed that Confederation would be _____ to Nova Scotia.
(advantage, disadvantage, advantages, disadvantages, advantageous, disadvantageous)

The Métis are of First Nations and European _____.
(ancestor, ancestors, ancestry, ancestral)

The Métis wanted to protect their traditional _____.
(culture, cultures, cultural, multicultural)

The _____ of Thomas Scott made many Canadians very angry.
(execute, executed, execution)

The _____ of Canada threatened the First Nations' way of life.
(expand, expanded, expansion)

The First Nations did not want to lose their _____ lands to the settlers.
(ancestor, ancestors, ancestry, ancestral)

Macdonald hoped that the National Policy would solve Canada's _____ problems.
(economy, economic, economize)

Macdonald was _____ in 1878.
(elect, elected, re-elect, re-elected, election)

The National Policy was intended to bring _____ to most Canadians.
(prosperous, prosperity)

The new tariffs helped to _____ Canada's economy.
(strong, stronger, strengthen, strongest)

Chinese _____ had to pay a head tax.
(immigrate, immigrant, immigrants, immigrate, immigrated)

The Mennonites came to Canada to escape _____ in Russia.
(discriminate, discriminated, discrimination)

Macdonald's _____ were not completely successful.
(politician, politicians, political, policy, policies)

EXPANSION OF THE COUNTRY: A

Crossword Puzzle

Work with your partner to complete this puzzle. Take turns reading your clues.

Across

2. Many of the railway workers came from this country.
6. The railway was _____ very quickly.
7. This is what the Métis wanted from the government.
10. Suffix: "person who ..."
12. This is how most Canadians thought of Louis Riel.
13. The Métis had a list of these.
17. Most Métis are the _____ of First Nations mothers and French or British fathers.
19. Prefix: "two."
22. These are the agreements that the First Nations signed.
26. This was a tax that the Chinese had to pay to come into Canada.
28. Noun form of "expand."
30. Past tense and past participle of "bring."
32. The Métis leader.
33. Prefix: "before."
35. Prefix: "not."
36. Prefix: "with" or "together."
37. This word means killing someone as a punishment.
39. A place where ships can load and unload cargo.
40. This word means "on horseback."

EXPANSION OF THE COUNTRY: B

Crossword Puzzle

Work with your partner to complete this puzzle. Take turns reading your clues.

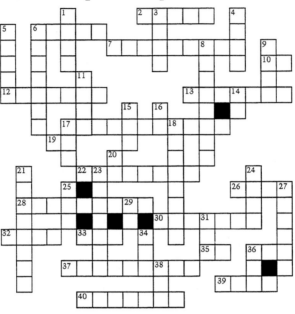

Down

1. This abstract noun suffix has an "i" in it.
3. This is how the Métis thought of Louis Riel.
4. Riel did this to save himself.
5. The name of the man who was executed by the Métis.
6. This animal was very important to the First Nations and Métis on the Prairies.
8. The Métis thought that Confederation would _____ their way of life.
9. Past tense and past participle of "sell."
11. This man wanted to take Nova Scotia out of Confederation.
14. Suffix: adjective.
15. This province joined Confederation to get a railway (initials).
16. Suffix: past tense.
17. Prefix: "not."
18. Abstract noun from "ancestor."
20. Prefix: "back" or "again."
21. You can add these at the beginning of words.
23. An area of land belonging to Canada's First Nations.
24. Past tense and past participle of "keep."
25. Suffix: "someone who..."
27. The Métis wanted to _____ their way of life.
29. Suffix: "person who ..."
31. Prefix: "one."
34. Suffix: "person who..."
36. The railway company.
38. This verb suffix has a "z" in it.

CANADA GROWS

Using Passive Verbs

Look at the highlighted verb in these sentences from the chapter and choose the correct meaning.

Some Canadian settlers attacked the Métis, but they **were captured**.
- ☐ *The settlers captured the Métis.*
- ☐ *The Métis captured the settlers.*

Later, one of these settlers, Thomas Scott, **was executed** by the Métis.
- ☐ *Thomas Scott executed the Métis.*
- ☐ *The Métis executed Thomas Scott.*

✔ *The Métis captured the settlers and executed Thomas Scott.*

*The highlighted verbs in the text are in the **passive voice**. The sentences are about the settlers and **what happened** to them after they attacked the Métis. By using the passive voice, the writer is able to keep "the settlers" as the **subject** of the sentence.*

Now look at this paragraph.

By 1911, there were only 769 Chinese women and 18 799 Chinese men in Canada. Chinese immigrants were unable to vote in elections in British Columbia after 1872. They **were discriminated against** economically and politically. In many cities in Canada, laws **were made** that stopped Chinese men from doing higher paying work; in some cities, laws **were made** that tried to stop Chinese people from living together. Canadians were afraid that Chinese immigrants would not fit in to Canadian society. Chinese citizens **were** not **allowed** to become full citizens with the right to vote until 1947.

In this paragraph, the writer uses the passive voice to describe what happened to the Chinese. Historians use the passive voice when nobody knows exactly who was responsible for what happened. Writers also use the passive voice when it may be uncomfortable to say exactly who was responsible. For example, if we ask who was responsible, the answer is "Canadians" or "the Canadian government."

To make a passive verb, we use this pattern:

Subject	A form of "be"	Past participle
Macdonald	**was**	**re-elected** in 1878.
The National Policy	**was**	**intended** to attract new immigrants.
First Nations People	**were**	**forced** to give up their land.
Railway track	**had to be**	**laid** across the mountains.
Chinese citizens	**were** not	**allowed** to vote until 1947.

Choose the correct form of a passive verb from the following list to complete these sentences containing information from Chapter 3.

attack	*discriminate*	*execute*
attract	*capture*	*finish*
promise	*sell*	*ask*

Rupert's Land _____ _____ to the Canadian government.

The Métis _____ not _____ for their opinions about adding Rupert's Land to Canada.

In Red River, the Métis _____ _____ by some Canadian settlers who supported the government of Canada.

During the conflict, a settler named Thomas Scott _____

_____ and _____ by the Métis.

The people of Prince Edward Island joined Confederation because they

_____ _____ a railway.

The railway _____ _____ six years early.

The Mennonites _____ _____ against in Russia.

Now, complete these paragraphs, using verbs from the lists.
Note: Not all these verbs need to be in the passive voice!

force   make   execute   think   order   create   elect   capture   attack

Some of the citizens in the North-West Territories _____ to support the government against Riel. A group of settlers _____ the Métis. Some of the settlers _____ by the Métis, and one of them _____. As a result of Scott's murder, many people in Ontario _____ that Riel was a traitor. But he was still a hero to the people of Red River and, in 1870, he and other Métis leaders _____ a deal with the government. As a result of this agreement, the province of Manitoba _____. Riel _____ to represent the people of Manitoba in the federal Parliament, but the people in Ontario wanted to _____ him for murder. Riel _____ to flee to the United States.

hire   stop   place   sell   strengthen   build   become   tax

American products _____ at very low prices in Canada. At the same time, Canadian products _____ in the United States, so Americans did not buy them. Macdonald _____ a new tariff on American-made products. As a result, American products _____ too expensive, and Canadians _____ buying them. The Canadian economy _____: more Canadian products _____; new factories _____; and new workers _____.

THE MÉTIS WANT SOME GUARANTEES

Read the following discussion between Riel and the Métis. Practise reading aloud.

PART 1: Riel and the Métis meet

RIEL: If you want me to help you, we must organize ourselves into a group. The new Canadian governor of the North-West Territories, William McDougall, has an army with him and they are coming here. The new Canadian government will listen to what we want if we are one group of people.

ENGLISH MÉTIS MAN: We need to decide if we want to join Confederation.

FRENCH AND ENGLISH MÉTIS: We will join only if the Canadian government protects our way of life. If it does not agree to protect our way of life, we will not join.

FRENCH MÉTIS WOMAN: The French Métis want the government of Canada to guarantee that we will be able to speak French and go to a Catholic church. We will join only if the Canadian government protects our culture. If it does not agree to protect our culture, we will not join.

RIEL: Then we have decided. We must meet McDougall and his Canadian army before they come onto our land. We must not let him take over the government of the territory. He must agree to our demands first.

FRENCH MÉTIS MAN: What do we do after we stop them from coming onto our land?

RIEL: We will set up our own government here in Fort Garry ... a Métis government. Our government will then make a deal with the Canadian government. We will have to make a list of things we want before we join Confederation. Agreed?

ENGLISH AND FRENCH MÉTIS: Agreed!

PART 2: The Métis and the government meet

Write a script for a discussion between representatives of the Métis and the Canadian government. Use some of the following expressions.

Asking for a Promise	Making a Promise
Can I rely on you to ...?	I promise that ...
Can I depend on you to ...?	I guarantee that ...
Can I count on you to ...?	I assure you that ...
Can I rely on that?	I give you my word that ...
Can I depend on that?	You can be sure that ...
Can I count on that?	You can count on me to ...
Do you promise that ...?	You can rely on me to ...
Do you guarantee that ...?	You can depend on me to ...

PROMISES, PROMISES

Look at the structure of this paragraph.

Main idea (topic sentence) **First example or detail**	The Canadian government made two sets of promises to achieve its goal of expanding Canada. **First**, the government made promises to Nova Scotia, the Hudson's Bay Company, the Métis, British Columbia and First Nations groups in order to persuade them to join
Another example or detail	Confederation. **Second**, after different groups of people decided to join Confederation, the National Policy made promises to make Canada a stronger country.
Conclusion or restatement	This is how Canada expanded.

Complete this paragraph, using information from Chapter 3.

Main idea (topic sentence) **First example or detail**	How did the government encourage people to join Confederation? **First**, the government promised to give Nova Scotia more _____ in return
Another example or detail	for joining. **Second**, the government promised to _____ Rupert's Land from the
Another example or detail	Hudson's Bay Company. **Third**, the government agreed
Another example or detail	to _____ the Métis way of life. **Fourth,** the government agreed to pay British Columbia's _____ and build a _____ from _____ to _____.
Another example or detail	**Next**, the government agreed to help Prince Edward
Another example or detail	Island _____. **Finally**, the government
Conclusion or restatement	signed treaties with the First Nations groups. **In the end**, it seemed that everyone got something in return for joining Confederation except the First Nations people, who lost their _____ of _____ and most of their _____ in the treaties they signed with the government.

SETTLEMENT OF THE WEST

Conflicts and Solutions in Western Canada

Conflicts between...	Cause(s)	Violence or negotiation?	Solutions?	Results: How did people feel about the solution?
First Nations and European settlers (¶7)				
First Nations and the Canadian government (¶8)				
Métis and the government's promises to the CPR and the Hudson's Bay Company (¶12)				
Métis and the Canadian government (¶3)				
European settlers and the CPR (¶17)				

Choices:
culture and values; lifestyle; needs and wants; how money should be used; communication.

Give some details:
e.g., rebellion, petitions, meetings...

LET GO OF YOUR DICTIONARY!

Using Context and Word Analysis to Infer the Meaning of New Words

If you use a dictionary to look up every word that is not familiar, you will slow down your reading. You may even reach the end of a sentence and forget how it started! Also, many English words change their meaning according to the context. For example, "product" has different meanings in mathematics, chemistry, economics and history. Outside school, the most common meaning for "product" is something on the supermarket shelf! Dictionaries don't know the context you are working in, so they may not give you the exact meaning you need.

The dictionary is a useful tool, but it's a good idea to try some other strategies before using it. Here are some suggestions:

- **Keep on reading** to see if you can understand the sentence or the paragraph without understanding exactly what this word means.
- **Infer the meaning from the context:** Look at the sentence and the paragraph and see if you can figure it out.
- **Analyse the word:** Does it seem to be related to other words you know? Are there parts of the word you recognize: base words; prefixes; suffixes?
- **Ask someone!**
- **If you are still stuck**, and if you really need to know this word in order to understand the sentence, use a dictionary. You will find an English learner's dictionary more helpful than a bilingual dictionary.

This activity helps you practise looking at words in context and inferring the meaning from the rest of the sentence or paragraph, or by using word analysis.

Find the paragraph in Chapter 4, read the word in context, and circle the best meaning:

	Word	Which meaning?	Clues
¶1	Benefit	Improve their lives Have problems Make money	Look at the previous sentence.

¶2	Transporting	Moving Moving up Moving across Moving down	Prefix "trans-."
¶7	Destroyed	Broken Killed Pulled down	The previous sentence.
¶9	Distrust	Opposite of trust Same as trust Hate	Prefix "dis-."
¶11	Surveyors	Look over Measure People who look over People who measure People who measure land	Read the rest of the sentence; suffix "-or"; look at the photograph on p. 48
¶11	Ignored	Did not listen to Did not include Did not notice Did not obey	Read the rest of the sentence.
¶11	Frustrated	Angry Unhappy Disappointed	How do you think they felt about the surveyors?
¶11	Ignoring	Not listening to Not including Not noticing Not obeying	Read the rest of the sentence.
¶12	Vacant	Free Empty Without people	Read the whole paragraph.
¶13	Petitions	Letters asking for something Letters Letters from a group asking the government to do something	Read the whole paragraph.

¶13	Respond	Answer Obey Listen Notice	Read the whole paragraph.
¶13	Concluded	Ended Inferred Decided	Read the whole paragraph.
¶13	Mistrust	Same as distrust Opposite of distrust Same as trust	Prefix "mis-": think of examples: "mistake," "misunderstand."
¶15	Recognize	Know Pay attention to	Read the rest of the sentence.
¶17	Freight rates	Transporting goods Cost of transporting goods Cost of goods	Read the previous sentence.
¶19	Negotiated	Made a deal Discussed the problem Argued	Remember what you read about Riel in Chapter 3.
¶22	Impatient	Upset Tired of waiting Angry	See the previous paragraph: how do you think they felt after all this time?
¶22	Rebellion	Fighting back Arguing Disagreeing Disobeying	Look at the pictures on p. 54.
¶23	Bankruptcy	A problem Danger A problem with money Losing all their money	"Saved" = "Rescued"; base word is "bank."
¶24	Were defeated	Lost Won	Read ¶¶24 and 25.
¶25	Treason	Murder Crime Disloyalty to Canada	Remember Chapter 3; relate this word to "traitor."

¶26	Opposed	Agreed with Disagreed with	Relate this word to "opposite."
¶27	Had ignored	Had not listened to Had not included Had not noticed Had not obeyed	Remember why the Métis became impatient.
¶28	Insane	Crazy Stupid Mistaken	What do you know about how lawyers sometimes try to save someone from punishment for a crime?
¶28	Mercy	Heavy punishment Light punishment	The word "but."
¶31	Profit	The money the farmers made The money the farmers lost Benefit Progress	The previous sentence

GREEK AND LATIN ROOTS

Do you ever feel that you can never learn all the words there are in English? You are right! English has more words than any other language, and nobody knows *all* of them.

Why does English have so many words?
This is because English has several **origins** or **roots**.

English has more words than any other language in the world!

English has borrowed words from other European languages, especially French.
Examples: *garage (French), piano (Italian), junta (Spanish).*

the roots of English

English has borrowed words from the languages of the areas that Britain colonized. For example, English includes words from the languages of North America's First Nations, especially for place names and the names of plants and animals.
Examples: *Canada, Toronto, Ottawa, tobacco, tomato, potato.*

Most of the everyday words and most of the grammar of English come from the Germanic language family of Northern Europe.
Examples: *man, woman, school.*

Most of the more academic and literary vocabulary comes from Latin and Ancient Greek.
Examples: *education (Latin), geometry (Greek).*

English also uses the Latin (or Roman) alphabet.

You have probably noticed that the language of textbooks is not the same as the language of everyday speech. One of the differences is that textbooks (and teachers too!) use an expanded vocabulary. They use many more long words!

Most of these words have Greek or Latin roots and it's really helpful to know some of these so that you can analyse new words. Many of the affixes you have learned are used with words of Latin or Greek origin. Here are some words that are related through a common root. In each family of words, you will find at least one that you have already read in *My Country, Our History*.

English words	Root	Meaning
rebellion; 'rebel; re'bel	belli (bellum)	fight
benefit; beneficial	bene	good
ancestor; succeed; successful; proceed	ced/ces (cedere)	go; follow
fact; factory; manufacture	fac (facere)	make, do
profit; profitable; benefit; beneficial	fic (facere)	made, done
transfer; infer; offer; suffer	fer (ferre)	carry
'conflict; con'flict	flict (fligere)	hit, strike
refugee; fugitive	fug (fugere)	run away, flee
geography; geometry	geo (gē)	earth
progress; aggression; aggressive; Congress	gress (gradus)	walk, go
graph; photograph; geograpy	graph (graphein)	write; draw
prejudice; judge; justice	jus (judicare)	law; right
located; local; location	loc (locus)	place
demand; command	mand (mandare)	order
major; majority	maj (major)	great, big
migrate; emigrate; immigrate; immigrant; immigration	migr (migrare)	move
origin; originate; original; Aboriginal	orig (origo)	beginning
politician; political; police; metropolitan	poli (polis)	city
populate; populated; population; popular	pop (populus)	people
port; transport; export; import; support; report; important	port (portare)	carry
oppose; opposite; position	pos (positio)	place
bankrupt; interrupt	rupt (rumpere)	break
sane; insane; sanitation; sanitary; insanitary	san (sanus)	health
ascend; descend; descendant	scend (scandere)	climb
solve; solution; resolve; resolution	solv (solvere)	loosen
stable; stabilize; stability; establish	stab (stabilis)	stand
construct; instruct; structure; destroy; destruction	struct (struere)	build
territory; territorial; Mediterranean	terra	land
attract; attractive; attraction	tract (trahere)	pull
urban; suburb; suburban	urbs (urbs)	city

Using what you know about affixes and roots, choose words from this list to complete the sentences:

benefit, beneficial   profit, profitable
justice, injustice   construct, destroy
population, populated, popular   emigrated, immigrated
rebel, rebellion, rebellious   attract, attractive, attraction
fugitive, fugitives

Chinese workers helped to _____ the railway.

The Chinese workers faced great _____; for example, they were paid less than other workers.

Louis Riel was a _____ against the government, but a hero to his people.

Dumont and some of the other leaders of the Rebellion became _____, but Riel gave himself up.

Was it _____ to hang Riel? Most English Canadians said yes, but many French Canadians said no.

After the execution of Riel, the government was not _____ among most French Canadians.

The National Policy was not _____ to Canada's First Nations.

At first, the new railway was not very _____; the settlers didn't want to pay the high freight rates that the CPR was charging.

The Homestead Act made Canada very _____ to new immigrants.

Millions of people _____ from Europe during the first years of this century.

SETTLEMENT OF THE WEST

If you analyse the way ideas are organized in a written text, you will find that the writer often makes a **general statement** about the main idea, then gives examples or details to support the statement.

Look at ¶2. Here is the structure of the paragraph:

Generalization:	The CPR would benefit ... **in several ways**. The government promised...
Example 1:	**This meant** ... would have to travel on the CPR.
Example 2:	The CPR would **also** make money transporting ... to the Prairies.
Example 3:	And **finally**, western farmers would have to use the CPR.

In ¶¶6-9, find the supporting examples. Note the concluding statement!

¶6: Generalization: ... increasing numbers of settlers ... made their lives much worse.

¶6: Example: _____

¶7: Example: _____

¶8: Example: _____

¶9: Example: _____

¶9: Conclusion: For all these reasons, the First Nations' distrust of the government grew.

Refer to the numbered paragraphs to find the generalizations, examples and conclusion:

¶10: Generalization: _____

¶11: Example: First of all, _____

¶12: Example: _____

¶13: Example: _____

¶13: Conclusion: Their mistrust of the government grew.

¶14: Generalization: _____

¶14: Example: _____

¶14: Example: _____

¶14: Example: _____

¶14: Conclusion: ... the settlers felt they did not have enough control ...

Note how ¶14 is related to ¶¶15-18! Paragraph 14 prepares the reader for what is coming next, and makes reading easier. Paragraph 15 expands on the first example, ¶1 on the second, and so on.

¶35: Generalization: _____

¶35: Example: _____

¶35: Example: _____

¶35: Example: Many of the Europeans were discriminated against.

¶35: Conclusion: _____

¶36: Generalization: _____

¶36: Example: _____

¶36: Example: _____

¶36: Example: _____

¶40: Generalization: _____

¶40: Example: _____

¶40: Example: _____

¶40: Example: _____

¶40: Example: _____

¶40: Conclusion: _____

PAST AND MORE PAST

Several time periods are covered in this chapter. The main context is 1885-1914, but the chapter also refers to events that happened before that. You read about some of these events in Chapter 3.

English uses two tenses to show the difference between an event that **happened in the past** and **something that happened even before the past event.**

For example, ¶7 says:

The different ways of life of the two groups **led** to another conflict. For many centuries the First Nations on the prairies **had depended** on following and hunting the buffalo.

<u>During the 1880s (simple past)</u>

<u>Before the 1880s (past perfect)</u>

Label these examples "during the 1880s" or "before the 1880s."

Before the building of the railway and the European settlement of the West, there **had been** about 20 million buffalo on the Prairies. By the 1880s, there **were** too few buffalo left to feed and clothe the First Nations people who **lived** on this land. Settlers and railway workers **had killed** the buffalo... The most important natural resource of the First Nations people on the Prairies **had been destroyed.**

_____

_____

_____

_____

_____

The tense that tells us "before that" is called the past perfect tense. To make the past perfect tense, follow this pattern:

subject	*had*	*past participle*
The First Nations people	had	depended on
Settlers and railway workers	had	killed the buffalo...

Refer to ¶¶8, 9, 10, 12, 19, 27 and 28 to see more examples.

Circle or underline the correct verb forms in the sentences. For example:

The First Nations people **were** (**had been**) here for thousands of years before the Europeans **arrived** (**had arrived**).

Many Canadians **wanted** (**had wanted**) Riel to be executed because the Métis **murdered** (**had murdered**) Thomas Scott.

Macdonald **was re-elected** (**had been re-elected**) in 1878 because of the promises he **made** (**had made**).

Although the Chinese railway workers **were** (**had been**) very important in the development of the West, the government **decided** (**had decided**) they were not needed after the railway was finished.

In 1884, Riel **returned** (**had returned**) from the United States, where he **fled** (**had fled**) after the conflict of 1870.

The Métis **became** (**had become**) very frustrated because the government **did not respond** (**had not responded**) to their petitions.

Businesspeople **invested** (**had invested**) in the building of the railway to make money, but by 1884 the CPR **was** (**had been**) almost bankrupt.

The railway **was built** (**had been built**) to make it easier to develop the West. By the 1890s, Canada **needed** (**had needed**) to attract new immigrants, and Sifton **looked** (**had looked**) for farmers from eastern and western Europe.

THE TRIAL OF LOUIS RIEL

*Louis Riel was **charged with treason** in Regina in July 1885. The lawyers that represented the government, the **Crown** lawyers, claimed that Riel had started the rebellion only to get money from the Canadian government. They also said that he was responsible for the deaths of many people. They asked the jury to find Riel guilty. The lawyers who represented Riel said that he was not guilty because he was insane. Riel disagreed with his own lawyers and said that he was not insane. The following dialogue is imaginary, but it is based on the arguments that Riel and his lawyers used in court.*

Riel's Lawyer: *(To the judge and jury)* Your Honour, Mr. Riel cannot be guilty of treason. He did not really know what he was doing. He is insane. Mr. Riel thought that he was doing God's work. Throughout the rebellion, he refused to carry a gun. Instead, he carried a crucifix! Mr. Riel was the leader of the rebellion, yes, but he did not know what he was doing. We cannot put him in jail or kill him for what he did. We must give him the medical treatment he needs to make him better.

Riel: *(To his lawyers)* Silence! I will not allow you to say that about me! I totally disagree.
(To the jury) Members of the jury, do not believe what my lawyers are telling you. I am a sane man. I knew what I was doing all along. The rebellion was not my fault. If Macdonald and his government had responded to the problems of the Métis and the Native people faster, the rebellion would not have happened. Macdonald is guilty of starting the rebellion, not me. Macdonald and his government knew of our problems and they ignored us. We were simply trying to defend ourselves.

Crown Lawyer: *(To a doctor)* Sir, after examining Mr. Riel, do you think that he knew what he was doing, or do you think that he is insane and did not know what he was doing?

Medical Doctor: *(To the Crown lawyer, jury and judge)* I believe that during the rebellion, Mr. Riel knew the difference between right and wrong. I think that Mr. Riel was sane at that time and because he knew what he was doing, he should be punished.

Judge: *(To the jury)* Members of the jury, please make your decision. You must decide if Mr. Riel is guilty or not. If Mr. Riel knew what he was doing was wrong, he is guilty. If Mr. Riel did not know what he was doing, he is innocent.

Innocent or guilty? You decide!

*The jury decided that Louis Riel was guilty and therefore should be executed. What would **you** decide?*

*Imagine that your small group is a jury of 12 members who must decide whether Riel is innocent or guilty. Discuss the case until you reach a **unanimous verdict**: everyone must agree.*

Use some of the following words and phrases to express your opinion and try to convince others on the jury to agree with you:

When you have a definite opinion...	When you are still thinking about it...
I think that...	I'm not sure that...
I believe that...	I'm not convinced that...
I feel that...	I'm not certain that...
I agree that...	I'm not positive that...
I am sure that...	
I am convinced that...	
I am certain that...	
I am positive that...	
I don't think that...	
I don't believe that...	
I don't feel that...	
I don't agree that...	

CANADIANS IN CONFLICT

Who chose to use violence to resolve conflicts?
Who chose to use peaceful negotiation?

This is the biography of one of the people who was involved in some of the conflict that you read about in Chapter 4. This is part of a jigsaw assignment for the class.

1. *Find the other people in the class who have the same biography.*
2. *Read the biography together and make sure you all understand it. Practise reading it aloud.*
3. *Write five questions about the biography. Check them with your teacher.*
4. *Return to your home group.*
5. *When it is your turn, read your biography aloud to the group.*
6. *Answer questions and explain anything that your group members did not understand. Re-read any parts that they did not understand.*
7. *Give the members of your home group the questions to answer. Then mark them and give them back with a copy of the biography so they can correct their answers if necessary.*

Wilfrid Laurier

Wilfrid Laurier was born in Quebec in 1841. He was a lawyer. Then he was elected to Parliament. He eventually became Canada's first Québécois Prime Minister.

Laurier was able to see both English and French **points of view**. He could speak both English and French and understood what both groups of people wanted and needed. In fact, if there were conflicts between French and English Canadians, Laurier often created solutions that satisfied both groups. Laurier believed that French Canadians should have the right to their language and culture. Laurier also thought that French Canadians should participate fully in the Canadian government in order to guarantee their rights.

*How do you think Laurier felt about the conflicts described in Chapter 4? Do you think he supported **violence** or **peaceful negotiation** to solve a conflict?*

CANADIANS IN CONFLICT

Who chose to use violence to resolve conflicts?
Who chose to use peaceful negotiation?

This is the biography of one of the people who was involved in some of the conflict that you read about in Chapter 4. This is part of a jigsaw assignment for the class.

1. *Find the other people in the class who have the same biography.*
2. *Read the biography together and make sure you all understand it. Practise reading it aloud.*
3. *Write five questions about the biography. Check them with your teacher.*
4. *Return to your home group.*
5. *When it is your turn, read your biography aloud to the group.*
6. *Answer questions and explain anything that your group members did not understand. Re-read any parts that they did not understand.*
7. *Give the members of your home group the questions to answer. Then mark them and give them back with a copy of the biography so they can correct their answers if necessary.*

Gabriel Dumont

Gabriel Dumont was born in Red River, Manitoba. He was a buffalo hunter, a farmer, a military leader, a **sharpshooter** and then an **entertainer**. The Métis people respected Dumont; many respected his courage, honesty and generosity. He was a very good military leader and soldier. In fact, he could shoot a duck's head from 100 m.

Dumont believed that the Canadian government would not try to solve the Métis problems. He felt that the Canadian government would ignore the Métis **unless** they used violence. He thought that the Métis should use violence to get the government's attention so that problems could be solved.

Dumont fought in the Métis rebellion. In the battle at Duck Lake, he was shot in the head but did not die. After the rebellion, Dumont became an entertainer. People came from far away to see his shooting ability.

*How do you think Dumont felt about the conflicts described in Chapter 4? Do you agree with his support of **violence**?*

CANADIANS IN CONFLICT

Who chose to use violence to resolve conflicts?
Who chose to use peaceful negotiation?

This is the biography of one of the people who was involved in some of the conflict that you read about in Chapter 4. This is part of a jigsaw assignment for the class.

1. *Find the other people in the class who have the same biography.*
2. *Read the biography together and make sure you all understand it. Practise reading it aloud.*
3. *Write five questions about the biography. Check them with your teacher.*
4. *Return to your home group.*
5. *When it is your turn, read your biography aloud to the group.*
6. *Answer questions and explain anything that your group members did not understand. Re-read any parts that they did not understand.*
7. *Give the members of your home group the questions to answer. Then mark them and give them back with a copy of the biography so they can correct their answers if necessary.*

Isapo-muxika (Crowfoot)

Crowfoot was born near Belly River, Alberta. He was a buffalo hunter, warrior and a leading chief of the Blackfoot Nation. In fact, he was the Blackfoot representative to the Treaty discussions with the Canadian government.

Crowfoot knew that more and more European settlers would come to the area where the Blackfoot lived. He believed that the Blackfoot people would have to change their lifestyle because of the settlers. However, Crowfoot did not believe that violence would solve the conflict between the Blackfoot and the settlers or the government. He refused to join the Rebellion. He thought an all-out war would bring disaster to his people.

*How do you think Crowfoot felt about the conflicts described in Chapter 4? Do you agree with his support of **peaceful negotiation**?*

CANADIANS IN CONFLICT

Who chose to use violence to resolve conflicts?
Who chose to use peaceful negotiation?

This is the biography of one of the people who was involved in some of the conflict that you read about in Chapter 4. This is part of a jigsaw assignment for the class.

1. *Find the other people in the class who have the same biography.*
2. *Read the biography together and make sure you all understand it. Practise reading it aloud.*
3. *Write five questions about the biography. Check them with your teacher.*
4. *Return to your home group.*
5. *When it is your turn, read your biography aloud to the group.*
6. *Answer questions and explain anything that your group members did not understand. Re-read any parts that they did not understand.*
7. *Give the members of your home group the questions to answer. Then mark them and give them back with a copy of the biography so they can correct their answers if necessary.*

Mistahimaskwa (Big Bear)

Big Bear was born near Fort Carlton, Saskatchewan. He was a buffalo hunter and a leader of the Cree Nation. He was proud of the Cree culture and way of life; he felt that Cree people should not be forced to give these up.

Big Bear did not believe that forcing the Cree to live on reservations was a good solution to the problem between his people and the European settlers and Canadian government. He tried to persuade his people to try to find a peaceful solution to the problem. Some of his followers disagreed with him and joined the Rebellion. The Canadian government blamed Big Bear.

After the Rebellion Big Bear gave himself up and asked for leniency for his people, not for himself. He was put in prison. He died shortly after he was freed.

*How do you think Big Bear felt about the conflicts described in Chapter 4? Do you agree with his support of **peaceful negotiation**?*

THE ALBERTA HOMESTEADER

Anonymous

My name is Dan Gold, an old bachelor I am,
I'm keeping old batch on an elegant plan.
You'll find me out here on Alberta's bush plain
A-starving to death on a government claim.

So come to Alberta, there's room for you all
Where the wind never ceases and the rain
   always falls,
Where the sun always sets and there it remains
Till we get frozen out on our government claims.

My house it is built of the natural soil,
My walls are erected according to Hoyle,
My roof has no pitch, it is level and plain,
And I always get wet when it happens to rain.

My clothes are all ragged, my language is rough,
My bread is case-hardened and solid and tough,
My dishes are scattered all over the room,
My floor gets afraid at the sight of a broom.

How happy I feel when I roll into bed,
The rattlesnake rattles a tune at my head.
The little mosquito devoid of all fear
Crawls over my face and into my ear.

The little bed-bug so cheerful and bright,
It keeps me up laughing two-thirds of the night,
And the smart little flea with tacks on his toes
Crawls up through my whiskers and tickles
   my nose.

You may try to raise wheat, you may try to
   raise rye,
You may stay there and live, you may stay
   there and die,
But as for myself, I'll no longer remain
A-starving to death on a government claim.

From *The Poets' Record: Verses on Canadian History* by Keith Wilson and Elva Motheral. Reprinted by permission of Peguis Publishers Limited, Winnipeg, Manitoba.

COMING TO CANADA: A JOURNAL

Read the case study, "The Immigrant Experience on the Prairies" (pp. 59-62). Then write in your own journal about your arrival in Canada. Write about your feelings, thoughts, opinions and experiences.

My Journey to Canada: *How did you travel to Canada? Were there many people? Was the journey comfortable? How was the food? How did you feel?*
Use p. 59, "The Ship over the Ocean," as a model.

Travelling inside Canada: *When you arrived in Canada, what was the first place you stayed? How did you get there from the airport? What sights, smells, tastes and sounds were new to you? How did you feel?*
Use p. 60, "The Train to Western Canada," as a model.

Food in Canada: *What foods were new to you in Canada? What customs were new to you? What did you like? What did you dislike?*
Use p. 60, "The Hotel," as a model.

My First Home in Canada: *Describe arriving at your first home in Canada. How did you feel when you saw it? What were you happy about? Were you disappointed? Was your new home in Canada different from your old home in another country? How was it different? How did you feel when you unpacked your belongings?*
Use p. 60, "The Homestead," as a model.

Home Improvements: *What did you do to your new home to make it comfortable? Did it feel "like home"?*
Use p. 61, "Building the House," as a model.

At School: *What was new to you at your first Canadian school? How did you feel when you saw it? What were you happy about? Were you disappointed? Was your new school in Canada different from your old school in another country? How was it different? Did you feel "at home"?*

My New Environment: *Did you like the weather, temperature and seasons in Canada when you first arrived? What did you like or dislike? Did you have any problems with the Canadian winter? Was the Canadian winter different from the winter of your homeland?*
Use p. 62, "Winter," as a model.

THE GROWTH OF CITIES: 1867-1913

The National Policy

promised that Canadians would have prosperity

... if more settlers came to Canada. How did this work out?	... if they had a railway across Canada. How did this work out?	...if American products were taxed. How did this work out?

↓ ↓ ↓

The Canadian population ☐ increased. ☐ decreased.	For Canadians, it became ☐ easier to buy Canadian goods. ☐ harder to buy Canadian goods.	Canadians bought ☐ more Canadian products. ☐ fewer Canadian products.

↘ ↓ ↙

Canadian industries needed to produce
☐ more goods.
☐ fewer goods.

↙ ↓ ↘

Canadian industries needed ☐ more material to make goods. ☐ less material to make goods.	Canadian industries needed ☐ more workers. ☐ fewer workers.	Canadian industries needed ☐ more factories. ☐ fewer factories.

↓ ↙ ↘ ↓

There were
☐ more jobs
☐ fewer jobs
for Canadians in rural areas;
for example, _____
_____
_____

There were
☐ more jobs
☐ fewer jobs
for Canadians in urban areas.

↓

Canadian cities became
☐ smaller.
☐ bigger.

USING THE GRAPHIC ORGANIZER

The graphic organizer you just completed shows some important changes that took place in Canada between 1867 and 1913. Many of these changes were the **result of** the National Policy. Many of these changes **led to** other changes.

Here are some expressions that tell us that an effect or result is coming next.

Cause		Effect
Macdonald created the National Policy	**in order to**	make Canada stronger.
Macdonald created the National Policy	**so that**	Canada would become stronger.
Macdonald created the National Policy.	**As a result,**	people bought more Canadian goods
The new tariffs	**meant that**	people bought more Canadian goods.
The new tariffs	**led to**	increased profits.
The new tariffs	**caused**	an increase in Canadian production.
The new railway was one	**cause of**	increased prosperity in Canada.

Here are some expressions that tell us that a cause is coming next.

Effect		Cause
Many immigrants settled in the West	**because**	the government offered free land.
Many immigrants settled in the West	**because of**	the government's offer of free land.
Many immigrants settled in the West	**as a result of**	Sifton's policy.

Use some of these expressions to make your own cause-and-effect statements about some of the ideas in the graphic organizer.

_____

_____

_____

_____

_____

_____

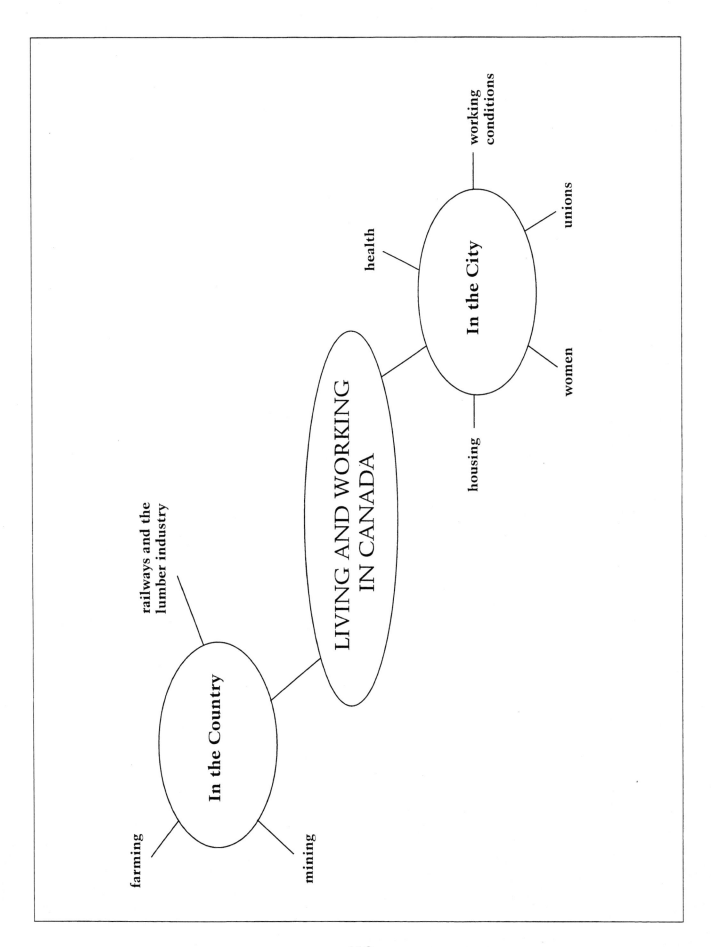

railways and the lumber industry

In the Country

farming

mining

LIVING AND WORKING IN CANADA

working conditions

unions

health

In the City

women

housing

USING THE GRAPHIC ORGANIZER

Use the information from the graphic organizer titled "Living and Working in Canada" to complete this paragraph that starts with a generalization and follows up with examples.

During the period between Confederation and World War I, living conditions in cities were very poor for working people. **For one thing**, people's homes were poorly built. **Also**, the homes were very crowded. **Another problem was** the lack of _____. **On top of all this**, people often suffered from disease because of _____ _____. **In fact**, Confederation did not improve the lives of most people in urban areas.

Here are some more generalizations about life during the period between Confederation and World War I.
Farm life remained much the same as it had before the National Policy was introduced.
Working conditions in the factories were very bad.
Workers in the resource industries had a hard life.

Choose one of these previous statements as a "topic sentence" to start a paragraph. Add examples and a concluding statement to complete the paragraph. Use some of these linking words to join your ideas.

For example	More examples	Last example	Conclusion/ summary/ restatement
For example, ...	Also, ...	Finally, ...	All in all, ...
For instance, ...	Another problem was...	Last but not least, ...	Overall, ...
One problem was ...		On top of all this ...	In fact, ...
First of all, ...	In addition ...		Indeed, ...
First, ...	Second ... (third, etc. ...)		
The worst problem was ...	Furthermore, ...		
	Moreover, ...		

EXPANDING YOUR VOCABULARY

Find these words or other forms of these words in the paragraphs indicated. Use the context and your knowledge of word roots and affixes to infer the meanings of the words:

¶10: luxury; locate;
¶11: sanitary; infect; insurance;
¶12: effect; standards; code; ignore;
¶14: season;
¶15: intimidate; deport;
¶16: compensate; contribute; financial;
¶23: legal;

¶24: hostile; militia;
¶26: private;
¶29: operate; supervise;
¶31: profession; encourage;
¶32 professor;
¶33: reluctant; experience;
¶34: accept; opportunity.

Use some of these words or other forms of these words to complete the following sentences.

Most Canadian cities developed in _____ that had natural resources and waterways or railways.

The factory owners usually lived in _____, but most of their employees lived in very crowded and _____ conditions.

It was _____ to join a union in Canada until 1872.

Employers were often _____ to negotiate with the unions. Sometimes they _____ their workers by threatening them with violence. Immigrant workers were sometimes _____ to their homelands if they complained about working conditions.

Laws were made so that injured employees would receive _____.

Women did not have many _____ to get a good education and most _____ were closed to women.

WHAT DO YOU SEE?

Making Observations and Inferences from Visual Information

You can learn a lot from the photographs and pictures in a textbook.

Look at the photograph at the top left on p. 67. Discuss these questions, giving reasons for your opinions and the inferences you make.

What do you see in the picture?

What do you see in the foreground? What inferences can you make?

What do you see in the background? What inferences can you make?

Do you think living conditions were easy for this woman and her family?

Do you think the house had running water or an inside toilet?

Do you think this house was warm in winter?

Where do you think the children's father is?

Look at the children's clothes and make some inferences about them.

Look at the people's expressions and the way they are standing or sitting and make some inferences about how they are feeling.

Look again. Is there anything you *don't* see? Does that tell you anything?

Now complete this description:

This is a photograph of a _____ family standing _____

their house in downtown Toronto at the turn of the century. There are

_____ children in the picture and one _____ who is

probably their _____. I think the children are between

_____ and _____ years old. The children's clothes

look _____ and they are all wearing _____, which

tells me that someone in the family has a _____.

The boy standing behind the others looks _____. The boy sitting

down looks _____. The girl seems to be _____, and

the youngest child is _____. The mother is not looking at the camera

because _____.

In the foreground are some of the objects that the family probably used. For

example, there are several large _____; I guess there is no

_____ in the house.

The house is in the _____ of the picture. It is made of

_____ and _____. It doesn't have many

_____ so there was probably not much _____ air in

the house. It was probably very _____ in winter and very

_____ in summer.

In this photograph, there are no natural features: no grass, no _____,

no _____, no _____, no _____.

The information in this photograph makes me think that life for most people at

the turn of the century was probably _____.

Now choose another photograph from this chapter and write about what you see
and the inferences you can make from what you see.

CHILDREN AT WORK

An Interview

In 1889, the government decided to investigate child labour in Canada. This is a transcript of an interview with a child who worked in a mill.

Q = Question   A = Answer

Q   What age are you?

A   I am 14 in August.

Q   Where do you work?

A   I work at Mr. Booth's mill at the Chaudière.

Q   How long have you been working in the mill?

A   Since the 25th of April I have been working in the mill.

Q   What were you working at last year in the box factory?

A   I was working on the butting-saw last year.

Q   What age would you be in August last?

A   Thirteen.

Q   What age were you when you commenced to work?

A   I was twelve and a half years old when I began this work.

Q   What hours do you work?

A   From six to twelve; then an hour for dinner — not quite an hour, because we start work again at five or ten minutes to one, and then we work until five past six at night. We quit work at six o'clock on Saturday.

Q   Are there any boys working there younger than you are?

A   Yes.

Q   What ages are they?

A   Eleven and twelve years of age.

WELL, YOU JUST WORKED HARD ...

An Interview

Barry Broadfoot is a Canadian writer who is very interested in oral history. He interviews people about their memories of earlier times or events in Canadian history. For one of his books, *The Pioneer Years: 1895-1914*, he interviewed people about life as a settler at the turn of the century. This is one of the interviews about life as a child on a farm.

Broadfoot did not include his questions in the book. In the interview that follows, look at the answers and write down what you think the questions might have been. For example:

What kind of childhood did you have on the farm?

One sure thing about those days, we sure knew how to work.

How old _____ when you first started to work on the farm?

Well, we used to have some jobs even before the age of five or six. It wasn't exactly that we called it work, it was more like just part of our lives.

What kind of work _____

Well, you never went between the barn and the house without picking up a load of wood for the fire. Even if you could only manage a few sticks you brought something. I've seen my two-year-old sister Mary toddling along with one little stick in her arms and getting a pat on the head from Mother.

What other jobs _____

We used to do things around the yard, hunting up hens and getting them back to the henhouse, and going for the cows with Spot, our dog, and handing my dad things when he was fixing a piece of machinery, oiling it, replacing a part that he'd fixed.

What _____ *in the summer?*

In the summer, I'd load up my little wagon with two jars, one of water and one of lemonade, and with sandwiches and cake and cookies I'd go out to the field where the men were working and give them afternoon lunch.

How different _____ *in those days?*

Oh, childhood was very different in those days. Well, we grew up fast in those days. I couldn't have been more than six when I put my childhood things away, my toys and my pets ... as we got older, we all got more responsibilities.

What special responsibilities _____

When I was seven or so there I was, winter or summer, milking my one cow, and then it got to be two cows and three, until by about nine I was doing a man's job with the cows, milking, carrying the pails to the house, getting the separator turning.

At what age _____ *school?*

Well, I didn't get much schooling. I was ploughing the fields at 11 years old, hardly big enough then to get the harness on, and me with a four-horse team, and at seven in the morning seeing all the other kids going down the roads to school, where I should have been going except Dad said the field had to be done, and that was that and I did it.

From *The Pioneer Years 1895-1914*, copyright © 1976 by Barry Broadfoot. Adapted by permission of Doubleday Canada Limited.

CHILDREN OF THE FACTORY

An Interview

In 1889, a special committee was established by the government to investigate working conditions in Canada. One of the people they interviewed was Thépile Charron, a young worker in a cigar factory.

The committee did not publish their questions. In the interview that follows, look at the answers and write what you think the questions might have been. For example:

Young man, what is your name?

My name is Thépile Charron.

Thank you. How old _____ now?

I just had my fourteenth birthday yesterday.

How long ago _____ work at the factory?

It's hard to believe that I first came to work at the cigar factory three years ago. It seems like only yesterday!

How much _____ when you started?

I earned $1 an hour as an apprentice.

And how much _____ now?

My wages are much better now. Today I am officially a journeyman cigar maker. On piecework, I have made as much as $4.45 in one week. I could probably make more money but we haven't been working our full hours lately. I wish we had more orders so that I could work my regular shift of 10 hours a day, 6 days a week. What else can a 14-year-old boy do with his time if he doesn't work?

When _____ *school?*

When _____ *games with your friends?*

Go to school? Play? That's only for the rich kids.

How many _____ *are working in the factory?*

There are a lot of boys and girls my age working in the cigar factory. We all work hard, but sometimes we get into trouble.

What kind of trouble _____

Only last week a supervisor walked by as two of my friends were cutting a tobacco leaf the wrong way. When he saw what they were doing, he hit them across the head with his fist.

What other kinds of punishment _____

The company doesn't like it if we talk while we work. If they catch you talking they make you pay a fine. I know someone who had to pay $3 in fines one week. Her wages that week were only $2. She ended the week owing the company money.

If the company bosses think you're wasting time, they put you into a place in the cellar they call the "black hole." Yesterday my best friend was put into that black hole. He told me that he was put into it in the afternoon and nobody let him out until 7 o'clock that night. He was really scared down there. There were no windows, no light, nothing. He thought they forgot that he was there when he heard everyone leaving the factory at the 6 o'clock closing time. He spent a bad hour until someone came back to let him out. I bet he'll never fool around at work again!

Adapted from *Curriculum: Working Language Skills* by permission of Centre for Labour Studies, Humber College and the Metro Toronto Labour Education Centre.

WOMEN WHO MADE A DIFFERENCE

How Will You Spend the Money?

A wealthy Canadian feminist has died and has left money in her will for projects that support women. You are the trustees of the will: you must decide how the money will be spent. Her will contains the following instructions:

Choose a project that will make a difference to women's lives or will encourage Canadian women today to make a difference.

Name the project after a woman who made a difference.

These projects have been suggested:

- An annual public lecture by a woman who is making a difference in Canada today.
- A women's health clinic.
- A university scholarship of $5,000 a year for the study of politics and women's history.
- A shelter for women and children who are victims of violence in their homes.
- An annual award of $5,000 to a woman in Canada who has made a difference.
- A film about a Canadian woman (or several women) who made a difference.
- If you prefer, you can choose any other project that all the trustees agree on.

The names of these women have been suggested:

- Emily Howard Stowe.
- Letitia Youmans.
- Flora MacDonald Denison.

Read the biographies of these three women.

Then choose a project and a name for the project.

Be ready to share your decision — and your reasons — with the class.

Emily Howard Stowe

Emily Howard Stowe was born in 1831 in Upper Canada. She was a teacher, a school principal, a university student and a doctor. Stowe strongly believed in education. In fact, after being a teacher and a principal, she decided to return to school to become a doctor even though it was difficult for women to do this. The University of Toronto would not acept her as a medical student because she was a woman, so she studied medicine in the United States. When she returned to Canada, she was forced to prac- tise medicine illegally, because the Canadian government did not license women doctors. Stowe finally got her licence in 1880. She was Canada's first woman doctor.

Letitia Youmans

Letitia Youmans was born in 1827 in Upper Canada. She believed very strongly that women were people who should and could change society. She felt that drinking alcohol was the cause of many social problems for men, women and children in families. She thought that drinking alcohol should be **banned** or made **illegal**. Youmans began an organization of women called the Woman's Christian Temperance Union (WCTU). Many women joined the WCTU because they agreed with Youmans. Many women suffered because their husbands and sons drank alcohol. The WCTU was one of the first organizations run by women. This organization was also one of the first places where women could voice their opinions and discuss their pro- blems openly. The WCTU persuaded the government to declare alcohol illegal for a few years during and after World War I. Most important, though, the WCTU showed that the problems, needs and wishes of women could get the attention of the Cana- dian government.

Flora MacDonald Denison

Flora Denison was born in 1867 in Ontario. Denison was a women's rights **activist**. She believed that women were treated unfairly in Canada. She believed that women should have the same rights as men and strongly supported the idea of **voting rights** for women. People who tried to gain the right to vote for women were called **suf- fragists.** Denison saw the change that she wanted finally happen in 1917 and 1918. Canadian women were given the right to vote in federal elections — a sign of political equality. Other forms of equality for women were still to come.

EQUALITY FOR CANADIAN WOMEN

Choose information from the biographies to complete the following paragraphs:

Topic sentence
Examples
Canadian women at the turn of the century were not equal to Canadian men. They were not allowed to _____ or to _____. Also, many Canadian women suffered from social problems caused by _____.

Topic sentence
Three women who changed life for Canadians were _____ _____, _____ and _____.

Details
Emily Stowe showed that women could _____ _____ .

Youmans and the WCTU showed Canadians that _____ was a serious social problem, and showed that women could _____ . Flora Denison helped women see that they could only gain equal rights if they had the right to _____.

Conclusion
As a result of the efforts of Canadian women like Stowe, Youman and Denison, the lives of Canadian women began to _____ at the turn of the century.

HOW DO YOU FEEL ABOUT WAR?

Survey the class and complete the chart. Use a checkmark (✔) for each answer.

	Yes	No	Not sure
1. Have you lived through a war?			
2. Would you go to war for Canada?			
3. Would you go to war for another country?			
4. Do you come from a country that has mandatory military service?			
5. Do you agree with mandatory military service?			
6. Do you think that war can resolve conflicts successfully?			

Use some of these expressions to complete the following statements about your survey.

many	most	the majority	a minority	only a few
several	quite a few	more than half	nearly all	none
hardly any	__ per cent	__ out of three	__ out of ten	all but one/two/three

_____ of the students in this class have lived through a war.

_____ of the students in this class would go to war for Canada.

_____ of the students in this class would go to war for another country.

_____ of the students in this class come from countries that have mandatory military service.

_____ of the students in this class agree with mandatory military service.

_____ of the students in this class believe that war can resolve conflicts successfully.

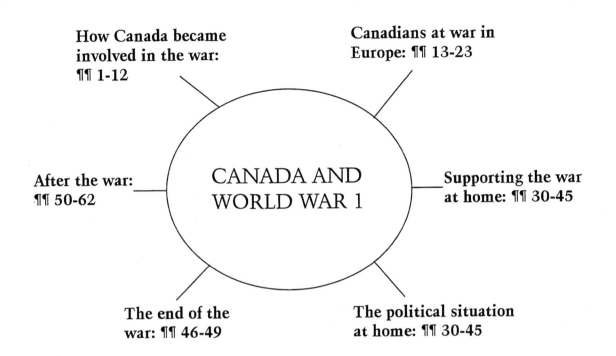

This is a long chapter with a lot of information.
The teacher will guide you through some sections.
Each person in the group will take responsibility for guiding his or her group through a section.
With your teacher, decide who will take responsibility for each section:

How Canada became involved in the war _____

Canadians at war in Europe _____

Supporting the war at home _____

The political situation at home _____

The end of the war _____

After the war _____

HOW DID CANADA BECOME INVOLVED IN THE WAR?

¶¶1-12

Write a cause of World War I in each box.

1.	2.	3.

4.

WAR!

Canada was a British colony; therefore,

How did Canadians feel about Canada's involvement in the war?
(Complete the following statements.)

Some Canadians . . .	Other Canadians . . .

Find these words in the text to see how they are used to express cause and effect.

To introduce a cause:	To introduce a result:

¶3 four reasons
      another cause
      a third cause
      the final cause
 	
¶5 because of
 	
¶10 As a result of
 	
¶11 because
	¶1 caused
	
	¶3 gave rise to
	
	¶4 led to
	
	¶5 so
	
	¶9 so
	
	¶10 therefore

Use some of these expressions to complete each of these cause-and-effect statements. Try to use a different expression in each one.

By 1914, the most powerful nations in Europe had plenty of weapons and strong armies and navies; _____, they were ready for war!

Imperialism _____ great competition among the powerful European nations.

Nationalism _____ war among the European nations.

Canada became involved in the war _____ the alliance system in Europe.

_____ Britain's declaration of war, Canada was automatically at war, too.

Some Canadians did not feel loyalty to Britain; _____, they did not support the idea of going to war for Britain.

Other Candians were eager to go to war _____ they thought it would be a great adventure.

CANADIANS AT WAR IN EUROPE

¶¶13-23

Topic	Main Ideas	Evidence/Explanation/Examples

The soldiers:

☐ They wanted to go
☐ They didn't want to go

☐ They were ready
☐ They were not ready

A soldier's life

What was a trench?

Life in the trenches

Canadian military contribution

Soldiers	1.	2.
RAF	3.	4.

Results?

1. _____

2. _____

SUPPORTING THE WAR AT HOME

¶¶24-29

Canadians at home worked on farms and in factories.
They produced

_____

_____

_____

for the soldiers.

Canadians at home consumed less.
They contributed

_____

_____

_____

to the war effort.

THE WAR EFFORT

Government policies supported the war effort.
These policies encouraged ...

1.

2.

3.

Women contributed to the war effort. They worked in ...

1.

2.

3.

4.

THE POLITICAL SITUATION AT HOME

¶¶30-45

THE WAR CREATED PROBLEMS AT HOME

Conflict between French and English Canadians	**Conflict between women and the government**	**Conflict between Canadian-born and immigrant Canadians**
Issues:	Issues:	Issues:
Solution:	Solutions:	Solutions:
Results:	Results:	Results:

"THE WAR TO END ALL WARS"
ended
at the eleventh hour
of the eleventh day
of the eleventh month:

November 11, 1918

How many served?
How many died?
How many were wounded?

What did Canada achieve?
Was it worth it?

AFTER THE WAR

¶¶50-62

Main Idea

The war was over, but ... THERE WAS STILL _____ IN CANADA

Subtopics

Between veterans and civilians	Between immigrants and other Canadians	Between workers and employers	Between farmers and the government	Between French and English Canadians

Details or Examples

Summary

1. The government _____

2. The economy _____

3. The people _____

Conclusion

The conflicts that surfaced during World War I would continue for many years.

CANADA AND WORLD WAR I

Understanding Words in Context

Find these words and choose the best meaning from the list on the right:

¶3: militarism   _____   a) the belief that some countries have the right to own others

      imperialism   _____   b) weapons and other equipment for war

      nationalism   _____   c) a group of nations that support each other

¶4: alliance   _____   d) willingly offered to go

¶5: allies   _____   e) winning a war or a battle

¶8: declared   _____   f) joining the armed forces

¶11: volunteered   _____   g) people who did not go to fight in the war

      war effort   _____   h) friends or supporters

¶12: opposed   _____   i) did not agree with

¶14: trenches   _____   j) supporting the culture or independence of a homeland

      artillery   _____   k) exploding weapons that were hidden under the ground

¶15 dug-outs   _____   l) heavy guns

¶21: victory   _____   m) forcing people to join the armed forces

      mines   _____   n) using armed force as a way of solving political problems

¶26: munitions   _____   o) made a formal announcement

¶32: enlistment   _____   p) the men who came back from fighting in a war

¶33: conscription   _____   q) freedom from fighting in the war

¶36: exemptions   _____   r) the place where soldiers stood to fire at the enemy

¶50: veterans   _____   s) the place where soldiers slept

      civilians   _____   t) working together to win the war

Use some of the words to complete these sentences.

English became a world language as a result of British _____.

_____ is as strong today as it was in 1914. For example, all over the world, groups of people are fighting to become separate nations, and many French Canadians in Québec would like to be independent of Canada.

Many immigrants in Canada have left their own countries because they don't agree with _____; they don't believe that armies should run countries.

At first, many young men _____ to join the army or navy because they thought the war would be short and a great adventure.

Most Canadians supported the war; people who _____ the war were not popular.

While the soldiers were fighting the war in Europe, people at home were also supporting the _____.

Many women worked in factories producing _____ for the armies in Europe.

Many Canadians did not have close ties with Britain or France and they did not agree that Borden should use _____ to force people to go to war.

Some young men did not have to go to war. The government gave them _____ because they were needed to work on the farms and produce food for the soldiers.

The arrival of the Americans helped the Allied Powers to win _____ in 1918.

Some _____ were very angry when they came home and found that there were not enough jobs for them.

CONSCRIPTION CROSSFIRE

Writing Letters to a Newspaper Editor

You are an English Canadian at the time of World War I. Write a letter to the editor of a French-Canadian newspaper, expressing your opinion about conscription. Persuade French Canadians to support the war. You can find some information in ¶¶31-34.

_____

_____

_____

_____, *1917.*

Dear Sir,

I am writing to express my opinion about Canada's role in the war.

I am very disappointed that _____

_____

_____

I believe that _____

_____

_____

I hope that _____

_____

_____

Sincerely,

_____

CONSCRIPTION CROSSFIRE

Writing Letters to a Newspaper Editor

You are a French Canadian at the time of World War I. Write a letter to the editor of an English-Canadian newspaper, expressing your opinion about conscription. You can find some information in ¶¶31-34.

_____

_____

_____

_____ , *1917.*

Dear Sir,

I am writing to express my opinion about Canada's role in the war.

I am very disappointed that _____

_____

_____

I believe that _____

_____

_____

I hope that _____

_____

_____

Sincerely,

_____

CANADIAN WAR POETRY

The Third Battle of Ypres

Raymond Souster

My old man dropped his piece of bread
in the Passchendaele mud, picked it up
again, wiped it off a little
and ate it. He stood in the water
to his waist at the guns
and stopped long enough from loading
to watch a fellow gunner
spin round three times before he fell
with his head blown off.
A shirt my mother sent him
he wore for three weeks
without changing it.
Finally it walked off his back.

None of this has ever
become part of history, which is
battles and generals. Well, those
   generals
tried hard enough to kill my father,
but he somehow escaped them.
Still, if he lives
a few years longer they may get him
   yet.

From *The Collected Poems of Raymond Souster*.
Reprinted by permission of Oberon Press.

War

Arthur Stringer

From hill to hill he harried me;
He stalked me day and night;
He neither knew nor hated me;
Nor his nor mine the fight.

He killed the man who stood by
   me;
For such they made his law;
Then foot by foot I fought to him.
Who neither knew nor saw.

I trained my rifle on his heart;
He leapt up in the air.
The screaming ball tore through his
   breast,
And lay embedded there.

Lay hot embedded there, and yet
Hissed home o'er hill and sea
Straight to the aching heart of one
Who'd wronged not mine nor me!

From *The Poets' Record: Verses on Canadian
History* by Keith Wilson and Elva Motheral.
Reprinted by permission of Peguis Publishers
Limited, Winnipeg, Manitoba.

GOOD TIMES AND BAD IN THE 1920s AND 1930s

Causes of the new prosperity

Good times in the 1920s

The effects on the lives of Canadians

Causes of the Depression

Bad times in the 1930s

The effects on the lives of Canadians

BOOM AND BUST: GOOD TIMES

Before reading this chapter, predict what you think is likely to happen in good times by completing this questionnaire.

Good Times . . . BOOM!

1. If you had a lot of money, would you . . .
   - ☐ buy things?
   - ☐ put money in the bank?

2. If your family had a lot of money and a house, would it be . . .
   - ☐ easier for your family to stay together in one place?
   - ☐ more difficult for your family to stay together in one place?

3. If you had a lot of money to spend, would factories, stores and other businesses have . . .
   - ☐ more business?
   - ☐ less business?

4. If factories, stores and businesses were busier, would there be . . .
   - ☐ more employed workers?
   - ☐ higher unemployment?

5. If all the farmland in Europe were destroyed in World War I, would Canadian farm products be . . .
   - ☐ in high demand?
   - ☐ in low demand?

6. If Canadian farmers could sell lots of their products, would they produce . . .
   - ☐ more?
   - ☐ less?

7. If your family and friends had jobs and houses, would you be more likely to . . .
   - ☐ re-elect the government?
   - ☐ want to change the government?

Now, compare your ideas about what happens in good times with those of your partner.

BOOM AND BUST: BAD TIMES

Before reading this chapter, predict what you think is likely to happen in bad times by completing this questionnaire.

Bad Times . . . BUST!

1. If you little or no money, would you . . .
   - ☐ buy things?
   - ☐ put money in the bank?

2. If your family had no money and no place to live, would it be . . .
   - ☐ easier for your family to stay together in one place?
   - ☐ more difficult for your family to stay together in one place?

3. If you had little or no money to spend, would factories, stores and other businesses have . . .
   - ☐ more business?
   - ☐ less business?

4. If factories, stores and businesses had fewer customers, would there be . . .
   - ☐ more employed workers?
   - ☐ higher unemployment?

5. If the weather were very dry in most of Canada's farming areas, would Canadian farmers produce . . .
   - ☐ more?
   - ☐ less?

6. If Canadian farmers could not sell a lot of their products, would they produce . . .
   - ☐ more?
   - ☐ less?

7. If your family and friends had no jobs and no homes, would you be more likely to . . .
   - ☐ re-elect the government?
   - ☐ want to change the government?

Now, compare your ideas about what happens in bad times with those of your partner.

WHAT WOULD HAPPEN IF ...?

Make some contrasting statements about what would happen in good times and bad times in Canada. Use some of the following words to introduce your statements:

To join ideas into one sentence:
..., whereas ...
..., but ...
..., although ...

To start a new sentence:
On the other hand, ...
However, ...
In contrast, ...

Examples:

Good times   If Canadians had a lot of money, they would buy more products, but
Bad times   they would probably put their money in the bank if they had little
              or no money.

Good times   If factories, stores and businesses had more buyers or customers, there
              would be more employed workers; however, if they had less business,
Bad times   unemployment would be higher.

Now, complete the following statements on your own.

Good times   If people _____ to spend,

                factories, stores, and other businesses _____

                _____

Bad times   _____

                _____

                _____

Good times   If Canadian farmers could sell _____

                _____

Bad times   _____

                _____

Good times   If most Canadians had jobs and homes, they _____

                _____ the government.

Bad times   _____

                _____

                _____

"WE'RE RICH!"

How the Stock Market Works

Share
Certificate

Wringer Washing Machine Company

The owner of this share certificate will receive a share of the Company's profits.

The Company will announce the exact amount of the profit that will be shared each year.

Signed: _[signature]_   Witnessed: _[signature]_

July 10, 1924

At the Shareholders' Meeting, 1925 ...

LIVING ON EASY STREET

As a result of new inventions, people could buy many new products in the 1920s. These products changed people's lives. Were the changes positive (+) or negative (–)? Give a reason for your opinion.

	New product	Changes in lifestyle	+ or –	Reason for your opinion
HOME CONVENIENCES	Refrigerator			
	Electric washing machine			
	Electric stove			
TRANSPORTATION				
COMMUNICATIONS AND ENTERTAINMENT				

BUY, BUY, BUY!

Writing Advertisements for New Products

Choose one of the new products that became available in the 1920s. Write a radio advertisement to persuade people to buy your product. Record your advertisement on audiotape.

Include:
- A name for the product that people will like.
- All the positive changes that buying one of your products would bring about in people's lives.
- An explanation that people do not have to pay all the money at once; buyers can pay monthly.
- A price.

Use some of the following expressions in your advertisement:

Promises

If you buy a _____, *you'll* _____.

If you don't buy a _____, *you* **won't** _____.

If you had a _____, *you* **would be able to** _____.

Persuasion
Hurry, hurry ....
Let's be honest ...
Don't waste your time ...
Don't be fooled ...
A lot of people out there ...
You've probably heard ...
These days ...
Time is precious ...
You want convenience ...
Buy now, pay later ...

1920s slang
It's the *cat's meow* ...   very attractive
It's *swell* ...   wonderful
He's a *big cheese* ...   a very important person
That's a *swanky* car...   very expensive
That's a *spiffy* dress...   popular and fashionable
That's *baloney*...   nonsense
That's *all bunk*...   nonsense

HOW EFFECTIVE IS YOUR ADVERTISEMENT?

First, listen to your own ad.

Use this checklist to help decide how effective your ad is.

Then, use the same checklist to help evaluate the ads created by other groups.

Your ad is effective if ...

	Needs work	Okay	Very good
Your pronunciation of all words is clear.	1	2	3
Other people can understand what you say.	1	2	3
You have included at least one statement beginning with "If ..."	1	2	3
You have included some of the language of persuasion.	1	2	3
You have included some 1920s slang.	1	2	3
You use language in a way that helps people remember your message; for example, you have repeated some words or expressions or used rhyme or songs.	1	2	3
Your advertisement is not too long.	1	2	3

HOW DID THE GREAT DEPRESSION AFFECT THE LIVES OF CANADIANS

Families: ¶¶26-29	Single Men: ¶30	Single Women: ¶¶30 and letter

As a result of the Great Depression ...

Immigrants: ¶¶31-34	Farmers: ¶¶33-36	Workers: ¶¶37-39

GOOD TIMES AND BAD

Idioms

Idioms are words and phrases that cannot be understood literally. For example, the word "boom!" describes the sound of a big explosion or crash, but "the boom years" in Canada were a time of great economic expansion and success.

When you meet an idiom like this, try to figure out the real meaning from the context. Find the following expressions in the text and match them with the best meaning.

¶1	boom years	_____	a)	real; believable
¶9	playing the stock market	_____	b)	sneak on to a train without paying
¶18	true-to-life	_____	c)	started being late with payments
¶19	big-spending	_____	d)	lost all their money
¶20	well-founded	_____	e)	had not expected something
¶21	went downhill	_____	f)	lost their jobs
¶23	went broke	_____	g)	think of a solution
¶24	go bankrupt	_____	h)	angry
¶25	laid off	_____	i)	spending lots of money
¶26	losing your shirt	_____	j)	investing money and taking risks
	fell into arrears	_____	k)	clothes that once belonged to someone else
	ended up on the street	_____	l)	a time when the economy is expanding
¶29	hand-me-downs	_____	m)	losing everything you own
¶30	ride the rods	_____	n)	lose all their money; be unable to pay bills
p. 104	roof over my head	_____	o)	became homeless
	cut down on	_____	p)	realistic; based on good reasons
¶33	money became tight	_____	q)	became much worse
¶41	had not seen (it) coming	_____	r)	use less
¶46	fed up	_____	s)	somewhere to live
¶50	come up with a plan	_____	t)	there was less money

ALL ABOUT ECONOMICS: A

Across

2. ¶22: taxes
5. ¶38: workers join these to support each other
8. ¶1: made it grow
9. ¶22: the money they had borrowed
10. ¶5: sell at a low enough cost to _____
11. ¶23: having no money
14. ¶22: desire for goods
15. ¶1: time when economy is growing
17. ¶8: ownership of part of a company
18. ¶26: payments that are behind
21. ¶2: sell to other countries
22. ¶21: a very bad time in the economy
25. ¶7: Figure 7.1: a drawing of the economic _____
26. ¶6: having plenty of money

ALL ABOUT ECONOMICS: B

Down

1. ¶22: sudden economic failure
3. ¶4: the money people put into a business
4. ¶22: products that are available for sale
6. ¶8: a share in a company
7. ¶1: started shrinking; became very bad
12. ¶24: unable to pay bills
13. ¶24: money owed to the banks or other people
16. ¶8: place where people buy and sell goods
17. ¶38: refusing to work
19. ¶3: goods that are ready for sale
20. ¶22: the amount of money that people earn
23. ¶24: pay back
24. ¶6: the amount of money a person earns in a week

CANADA AND WORLD WAR II

How Canada became involved in the war: ¶¶1-19	How Canadians felt about the war: ¶¶20-29
Canadians at war in Europe and Asia: ¶¶34-38	Supporting the war at home: ¶¶39-44
How the war changed Canadian society: ¶¶45-53	The political and economic effects of the war: ¶¶54-end

FROM ONE WORLD WAR TO ANOTHER

The Causes of World War II

This chart summarizes the main causes of World War II, but the examples and consequences do not match! Use the blank chart to reorganize the information.

Causes	Examples, reasons and/or results	Consequences
¶5: Some countries in Europe became dictatorships. It was dangerous to disagree with the government in these countries.	The size of the German navy and army was reduced. Britain and France did not want to fight any more wars; they wanted to settle all conflicts peacefully.	Aggressive countries were not stopped from invading and taking over other countries around them.
¶6: The Treaty of Versailles forced the losers of World War I to give up parts of their land to form new countries.	Benito Mussolini became a dictator in Italy. Soldiers from the countries that won the war occupied parts of Germany.	These governments developed aggressive policies to make their countries strong.
¶¶7-10: Germany felt humiliated after losing World War I and being forced to conform to the terms of the Treaty of Versailles.	A new government led by Adolf Hitler and the Nazi Party came to power in Germany. German people were separated and living in different countries.	Germany wanted revenge against the countries that won World War I.
¶¶13-16: The League of Nations failed to keep peace among all nations.	The Soviet Union had a very strong leader, Josef Stalin.	Germans felt angry; they wanted their land back so that all Germans could live in the same nation.

FROM ONE WORLD WAR TO ANOTHER

The Causes of World War II

Causes	Examples, reasons and/or results	Consequences
¶5: Some countries in Europe became dictatorships. It was dangerous to disagree with the government in these countries.		
¶6: The Treaty of Versailles forced the losers of World War I to give up parts of their land to form new countries.		
¶¶7-10: Germany felt humiliated after losing World War I and being forced to conform to the terms of the Treaty of Versailles.		
¶¶13-16: The League of Nations failed to keep peace among all nations.		

THE CAUSES OF WORLD WAR II

Writing Paragraphs Showing Cause and Effect

Read the following paragraph. It is a summary of the causes of World War II, based on the information in the chart titled "From One World War to Another."

Topic sentence and first detail	There were **four major causes** of World War II. **One was** the new forms of government in Europe. **Another was** the treaty of Versailles. **A third factor was** the humiliation of Germany after World War I. **The last major cause of the war was** the failure of the League of Nations.
Another detail	
Another detail	
Last detail	

Notice this technique:
Some of the language from the chart has been changed to make it fit the structure of the paragraph. For example, some verbs have been changed to nouns:

Germany **felt humiliated...** — ...the **humiliation** of Germany ...
The League of Nations **failed...** — ...the **failure** of the League of Nations...

Work together to write an essay about the causes of World War II. Start with the sample paragraph on this page. Then each group member can contribute a paragraph explaining one of the major causes of the war, using information from the chart "From One World War to Another."

Choose one of these topic sentences:

One of the major causes of World War II was the ... that did not allow ...
Another cause of the Second World War was the ..., which forced ...
A third factor was the humiliation of Germany ...
Finally, the League of Nations' failure to ... **also contributed to** ...

Use some of the following words and expressions when you construct your paragraph:

Introduce examples or details

For example, ...
For instance, ...
First of all,
One example was ...
One result was ...
One reason was ...
Another ...
Second, ...
Third, ...
Also, ...

Explain the results or consequence

As a result, ...
Therefore, ...
Consequently, ...
As a consequence, ...
The result was ...

Now, copy the opening paragraph, beginning "There were four major causes... ."

Add your own paragraphs in the correct order.

Check each other's grammar and spelling and make sure that you have not used the same words or expressions too many times.

Add a concluding paragraph (one or two sentences) restating or summarizing the main idea of the first paragraph. You may wish to use the following sentence openers:

These were the major causes...
War broke out on ...

Congratulations! You have written an essay!

SHOULD WE GO TO WAR AGAIN?

At the beginning of World War I, many Canadians had been enthusiastic about going to war. But public opinion about World War II was very different. Canadians remembered their experiences during and after World War I. Many people thought it was not wise to go to war again.

Complete the following statements about public opinion in Canada in 1939. Paraphrase the main points: do not use the same words as the text! For example:

The text: They thought that the government should be using its money to create jobs and help the poor, not to fight a war in Europe.

Paraphrase: *Some Canadians felt that the government should help Canadians at home instead of spending money on war.*

Some people _____ that the Allies had _____ the

Germans _____ after _____.

The Prime Minister felt that war _____ among

Canadians.

Many French Canadians _____ because

_____.

Many people who had jobs felt it was more important to _____ than

to _____.

Canadians remembered the people who _____ in World War I; they

did not want _____.

Many English Canadians believed that _____;

therefore, Canadians should _____ in the war.

SHOULD CANADA GO TO WAR AGAIN?

Consider the opinions for and against war.
What would happen if Canada went to war again?

Consider the following issues:
- the cost in money.
- the cost in lives.
- the conflicts created.
- the growth and development of industry.
- the growth and development of agriculture and fisheries.
- the development or changes in government.

Imagine you are a Canadian in 1939.
What is your decision?

Weigh the advantages and disadvantages:

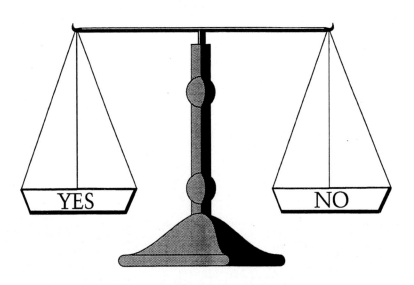

ALLONS-Y CANADIENS!

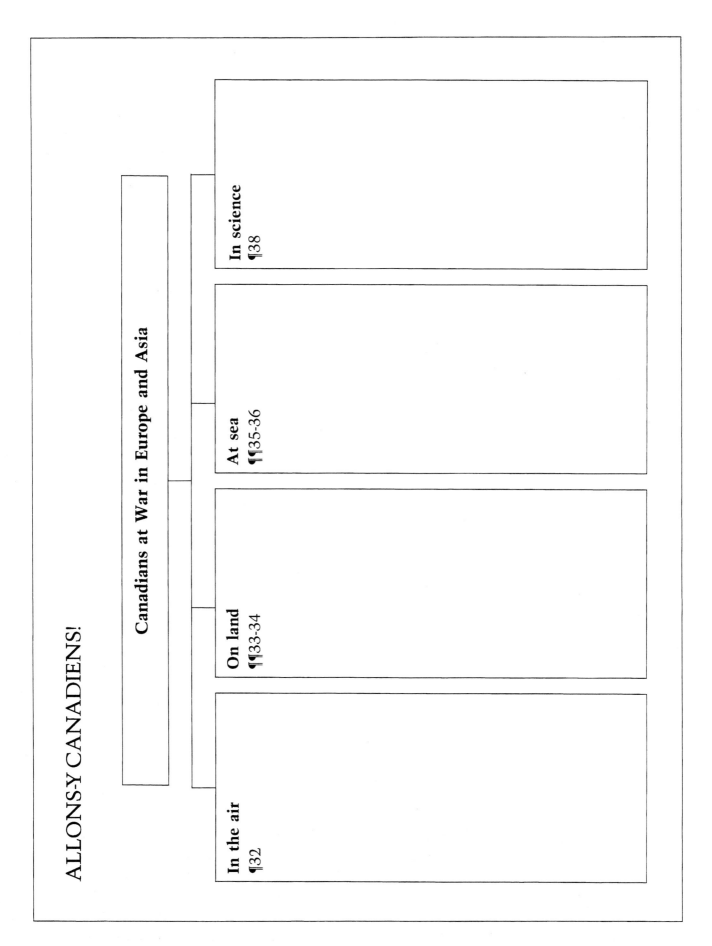

Canadians at War in Europe and Asia

In science
¶38

At sea
¶¶35-36

On land
¶¶33-34

In the air
¶32

ALLONS-Y CANADIENS!

Supporting the War at Home

Industries
¶40

Food production
¶41

Personal efforts
¶42

Government
¶¶43-44

HOW THE WAR CHANGED CANADIAN SOCIETY

	How did society change?	Examples, details
The role of government ¶¶46-47	Before the war, the government did not think it was its responsibility to look after the basic needs of Canadians. After the war, the Canadian government became much more involved in taking care of Canadians.	
Women ¶¶48-51		
Immigrants ¶¶52-53		

THE POLITICAL AND ECONOMIC EFFECTS OF THE WAR

	How did society change?	Examples, details
The economy ¶55	The war effort caused industrial expansion and the end of the Depression.	
Canada and the world ¶56		
The costs ¶57		

LET GO OF YOUR DICTIONARY!

Part One

You probably found a lot of unfamiliar words in this chapter. How did you deal with them? You probably used one of the following strategies:

Use Context to Infer Meaning
The context may help you understand the word. For example, in ¶5, you can figure out the meaning of "**humiliated**" by looking at the previous sentence. Many Germans felt that their pride as a nation had been damaged. "**Humiliated**" probably means the opposite of "proud."

Don't forget that context clues may include pictures as well as text!

Okay? Keep reading!

Didn't help? Try this!

Analyse the Word
If the context doesn't help you, try to analyse the words: look at the parts of the word and relate them to others that you know. For example, in ¶8, "**imprison**," is related to the word "**prison**," and the prefix "**im**" often means "in" (e.g., "import"). Therefore, this word has something to do with "in prison." You can tell from the way it is used in the sentence that it is a verb; so **imprison** probably means "put someone in prison."

Okay? Keep reading!

Didn't help? Try this!

Use Your Dictionary!
Use your dictionary only when you are stuck and when you have no other source of help — for example, when you are studying at home. If you stop to look up every word, you will slow down your reading and you will probably lose the main idea.

Didn't help? Try this!

Ask Someone!
If you are still stuck, ask your teacher.

Okay? Keep reading!

LET GO OF YOUR DICTIONARY!

Part Two

Here is a list of words from Chapter 8. How did you find the meanings?

In the column on the right, write *K* if you already knew the words, *I* if you used the context to figure out the meaning, *A* if you analysed the parts of the word or related the word to other words you know, *?* if you asked someone, and *D* if you used a dictionary.

¶5	condition	_____	¶38	atomic bomb	_____
	bitterly	_____		destruction	_____
	revenge	_____	¶40	plants	_____
¶8	cheated	_____		vast quantities	_____
	dictator	_____	¶41	grain	_____
¶9	persecuted	_____	¶42	gave up	_____
¶14	appeasement	_____		parachutes	_____
¶24	reconsider	_____		rationing	_____
¶26	*blitzkreig*	_____		coupons	_____
	occupied	_____	¶43	aspects	_____
	regimes	_____		vehicles	_____
¶28	Aryans	_____		give notice	_____
	inferior	_____	¶45	basic needs	_____
¶32	invade	_____		ethnic minority	_____
¶33	garrison	_____	¶46	role	_____
	surrender	_____	¶47	recession	_____
	disaster	_____		Unemployment Insurance	_____
	landing craft	_____		Family Allowance	_____
	tanks	_____	¶50	keep their spirits up	_____
¶34	defeats	_____	¶52	internment camps	_____
¶35	U-boats	_____	¶53	confiscated	_____
	submarines	_____		generations	_____
¶37	suicide	_____	¶58	counselling	_____

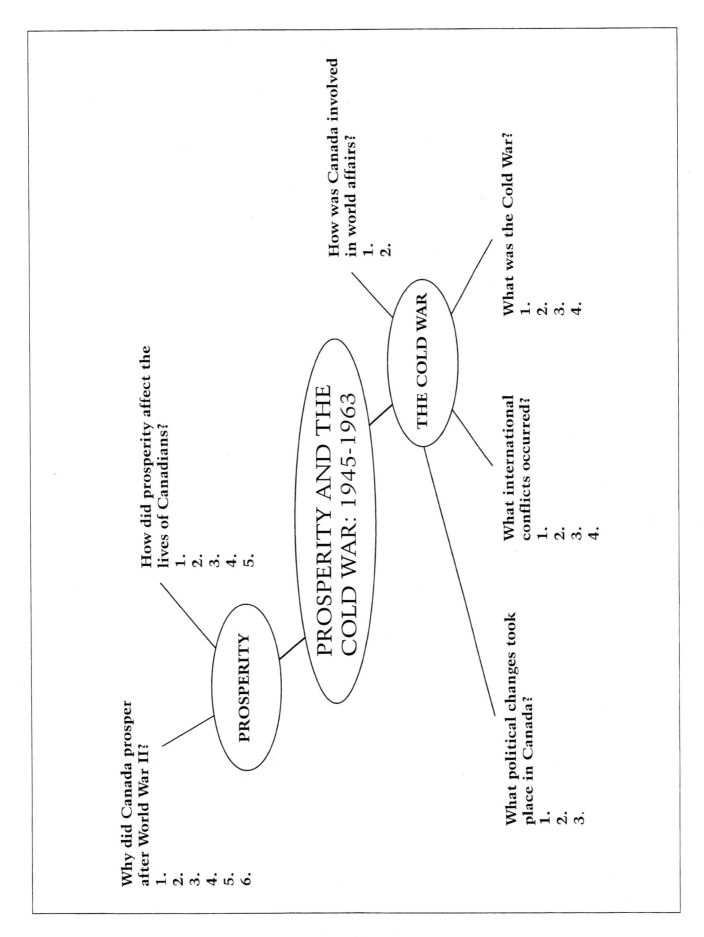

Why did Canada prosper
after World War II?
1.
2.
3.
4.
5.
6.

PROSPERITY

How did prosperity affect the
lives of Canadians?
1.
2.
3.
4.
5.

PROSPERITY AND THE
COLD WAR: 1945-1963

THE COLD WAR

How was Canada involved
in world affairs?
1.
2.

What was the Cold War?
1.
2.
3.
4.

What international
conflicts occurred?
1.
2.
3.
4.

What political changes took
place in Canada?
1.
2.
3.

PROSPERITY COMES TO CANADA AGAIN!

¶¶3-5 **The government stimulated the economy**
by creating tax deductions.

by selling _____

and by helping _____

¶¶6-7 **Unions stimulated the economy**

by helping workers get better _____

and _____

¶8 **Consumers stimulated the economy**

by _____

¶¶9-11 **Immigration stimulated the economy**

by bringing more _____

and more _____ to Canada.

¶12 **The "baby boom" stimulated the economy**

by creating new _____

¶13 **American investment stimulated the economy**

by _____

CANADIAN PROSPERITY

HOW DID PROSPERITY AFFECT LIFE IN CANADA?

Read ¶¶14-24 and complete these statements of cause and effect.

Canadian cities grew rapidly after the war; as a result, _____

_____. Homes were built in the suburbs because _____

_____. People who lived in the suburbs had to travel farther to work;

therefore, _____.

Canadians bought many new products, such as _____,

_____, and _____, in order to _____

_____.

Workers had better _____, better _____ and more

_____. This meant that _____

_____.

There were more children after the war. As a consequence, _____

_____.

Canadian teenagers had money to spend. They contributed to the boom by ____

_____.

The Massey Commission was created in 1949 because the government _____

_____.

The Canada Council was created in order to _____

_____.

THE LIFE OF A TEENAGER IN THE 1950s AND TODAY

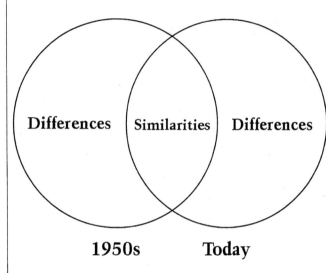

1950s   Today

This is a Venn diagram. It is used to show how two things are the same and different.

Make a Venn diagram of your topic to show how the life of a Canadian teenager today is the same as or different from the life of a Canadian teenager in the 1950s.

Then, use the information from the completed chart to write some sentences about similarities and differences. You can use some of the following expressions:

Similarities

Young people in the 1950s used to ..., **and** they do today, **too**.

Today, **just as** in the 1950s, teachers ...

In the 1950s, Canadian teenagers used to ... **Similarly**, teenagers today ...

One thing that schools today have **in common** with schools in the 1950s is ...

... was very popular in the 1950s. **Likewise**, teenagers today enjoy ...

Differences

High school students in the 1950s had to ..., **but** they don't today.

Teenagers in the 1950s had **more (less, fewer) ... than** teenagers today.

In the 1950s, Canadian teenagers used to ... **whereas** today, they ...

School was very ... in the 1950s. **In contrast**, schools today ...

Teenagers today are **not as ... as** teenagers in the 1950s.

Unlike teachers in the 1950s, teachers today ...

HOW WAS CANADA INVOLVED IN WORLD AFFAIRS?

Read ¶¶26-34. Then, label the map showing how Canada and other nations of the world formed new alliances after the war. Use some of these words and phrases:

Canada	protect	hostile	Western European
capitalist	United Nations	communist	Eastern European
France	Britain	different	Cold
United States	preserve	Soviet Union	alliance
		nuclear	

The _____ _____ was created to _____ peace, but ...

The _____ World   The _____ World

????
_____ political systems
_____ relationships
_____ bombs
_____ War
????

to _____ themselves, each side
formed a new _____

NATO

The _____ _____,
_____,
_____,
_____, and eight
other _____
_____ countries
(nine in 1983).

The Warsaw Pact

The _____ _____
and seven other _____
countries.

CANADA'S INVOLVEMENT IN WORLD AFFAIRS

Decide whether each of the following statements is true or false. Support your choice by paraphrasing information from the text. The first one is completed for you.

¶27: Canada remained closely tied to Britain after the war.
This is false. Canada became more closely tied to the United States after the war.

¶29: The Cold War was based on different political ideas.
This is _____. _____
_____

¶31: During the Cold War people were afraid of nuclear war.
This is _____. _____
_____

¶34: NATO was formed as a result of the Warsaw Pact.
This is _____. _____
_____

¶¶35-36: Canada supported South Korea during the Korean War.
This is _____. _____
_____

¶¶37-42: The Suez Crisis started because the British and French wanted to build a canal.
This is _____. _____
_____

¶¶46-48: Canada supported the United States during the Cuban Missile Crisis.
This is _____. _____
_____

GOVERNMENTS IN THE WORLD TODAY

Make a chart like this to record the kinds of political and economic systems that exist in the countries that some of your classmates come from.

Country	Political system	Economic system
Canada	Democracy. Everyone over 18 has a vote. There are several political parties.	Capitalist. Individuals and corporations may own businesses, banks and land. Everyone pays taxes to fund public services.

Choose someone from a country that has a different type of government from Canada's and interview him or her about the government's role in some aspects of life in that country. Here are some topics you might find out about:

How the government is chosen
Public services (e.g., education, health, water, roads, etc.)
Taxes
The role of the armed forces and the police
Land ownership and farming
Business
The press (TV, radio, newspapers)
Culture (music, dance, clothing)
Family life
Jobs and income
Human rights

HOW DID CANADIANS VOTE?

Use the election results shown on pp. 159, 160 and 161 to complete the chart.

	1957	1958	1962	1963
Progressive Conservatives				
Liberals				
CCF (NDP)				
Social Credit				
Others				
	265	265	265	265

Complete the following statements, using the names of the political parties and the words "minority government" or "majority government."

The _____ formed a _____

in 1957. The _____ formed the opposition.

The _____ formed a _____

in 1958. The _____ formed the opposition.

The _____ formed a _____

in 1962. The _____ formed the opposition.

The _____ formed a _____

in 1963. The _____ formed the opposition.

FRENCH-ENGLISH RELATIONS IN CANADA

Tensions and conflicts between French and English Canadians have existed throughout Canadian history. You have already read about some of the causes of these tensions and conflicts in earlier chapters. Reviewing some of that information will help you prepare to read Chapter 10.

Complete these paragraphs, using examples and details drawn from earlier chapters in the text.

Chapter 3, ¶¶4-13 French Canadians have felt that they might be in danger of losing their culture.	**Chapter 4, ¶¶10-25** French Canadians have not always trusted the government.	**Chapter 6, ¶¶30-36** and **Chapter 8, ¶¶24-29** English and French Canadians have disagreed over the issue of conscription during wartime.
↓	↓	↓

Tensions and conflicts still exist between English and French Canada.

POLITICAL CONFLICTS IN CANADA

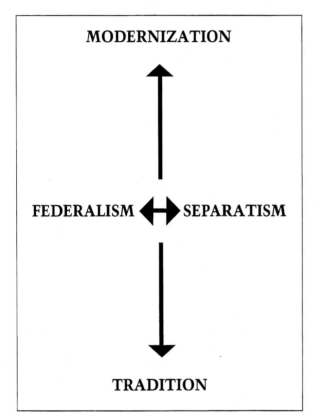

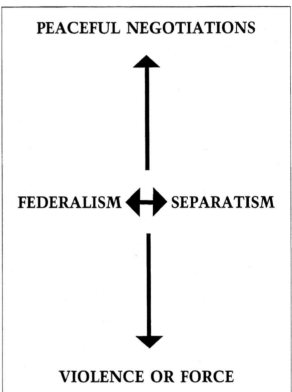

Where do they fit?

Trudeau (Liberal)   Lesage (Liberal)

Duplessis (Union Nationale)   FLQ

Lévesque (Parti Québécois)   Pearson (Liberal)

WHAT DID THEY BELIEVE?

Different politicians and political groups had different ideas and beliefs about how Quebec should relate to the rest of Canada and how Quebec could have a good future.

Find information in the text (¶¶5-27) to complete the following paragraphs about the beliefs of these politicians.

Maurice Duplessis believed that Quebec should keep a _____ way of life. He also believed that the federal government should _____ Quebec politics. Duplessis believed in using _____ against people who opposed his government. For example, _____

_____

_____

_____

Jean Lesage believed that Quebec should _____ its economy and _____ its culture. For example, _____

_____

_____. Also, _____

_____

_____

Now write paragraphs of your own describing the beliefs of each of the following politicians or groups.

Lester Pearson (Liberal)   René Lévesque (Parti Québécois)
Pierre Trudeau (Liberal)   FLQ: Front de Libération du Québec

THE OCTOBER CRISIS: NEWSPAPER HEADLINES

Refer to ¶¶28-32 to complete the news headlines about events that took place in Canada in October 1970. Notice that the present tense is used in headlines, even though the article is about events that took place in the past (usually the day before the newspaper is printed). Notice also that headlines often omit some words; especially "the," "a," "is" and "are."

FLQ Kidnaps British Diplomat _____ _____ in _____

FLQ _____ Pierre Laporte, _____ _____ of Quebec

Quebec Premier Bourassa _____ Federal Government for _____

Trudeau _____ War _____ Act

Canadian Army _____ Streets, _____ Public Buildings

Police _____ New Powers

Pierre Laporte's Body _____ in _____ of _____

Cross's Kidnappers _____ to Cuba

Laporte's Kidnappers _____ of _____,
_____ to Life in Prison

436 people _____ under War Measures Act

20 people _____ of Crimes in Quebec Terrorism

CONSTITUTIONAL CROSSFIRE

Canada's Constitution and Charter of Rights and Freedoms are documents that clearly state:

- The powers of the Federal Government.
- The powers of the provincial governments.
- The rights and freedoms of all Canadians.

When the federal government wanted to change the Constitution in 1982 and 1992, it created many conflicts.

Read ¶¶43-55 to find the causes of these conflicts and the solutions or results. Make notes (one or two words) in each box below.

Conflicts	1982 Constitutional Changes		1992 Constitutional Changes	
	Causes of conflict	Solutions or results	Causes of conflict	Solutions or results
Between provinces and federal government	¶45	¶46	¶54	¶55
Between some provinces and women	¶45	¶47		
Between some provinces and Native groups	¶45	¶47	¶54	¶55
Between some provinces and French Canadians	¶45	¶47	¶54	¶55
Between Quebec and the federal government	¶49	¶49-50	¶54	¶55
Between Westerners and the federal government			¶54	¶55
Between Canadians in Atlantic provinces and the federal government			¶54	¶55

CREATE A CROSSWORD!

Puzzle A

The answers to this puzzle are filled in for you — but you need to write the clues. If two group members team up to write the Across clues and two work together to write the Down clues, you can trade your clues and a blank grid with a group that is working on Puzzle B. Your clues should be based on the content of Chapter 10 and should include a paragraph reference.

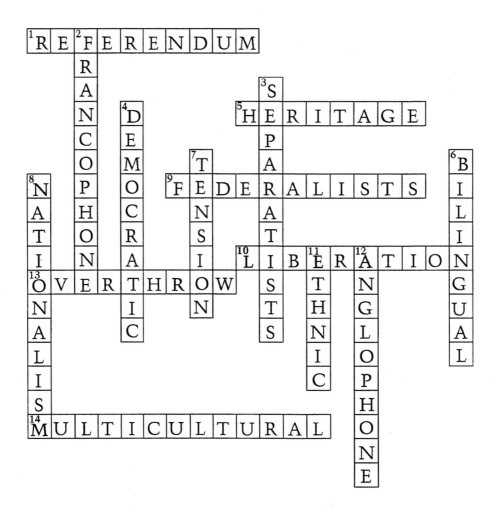

CREATE A CROSSWORD!

Puzzle A

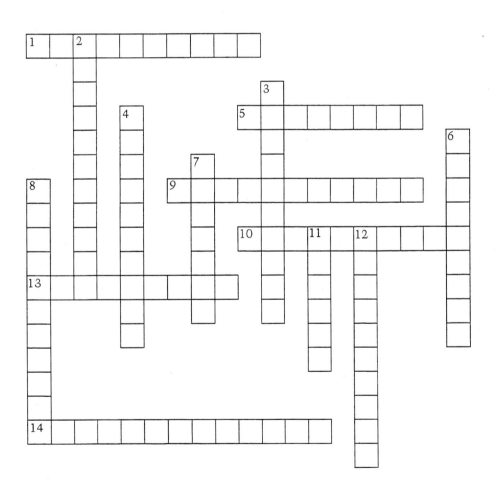

CREATE A CROSSWORD!

Puzzle B

The answers to this puzzle are filled in for you — but you need to write the clues. If two group members team up to write the Across clues and two work together to write the Down clues, you can trade your clues and a blank grid with a group that is working on Puzzle B. Your clues should be based on the content of Chapter 10 and should include a paragraph reference.

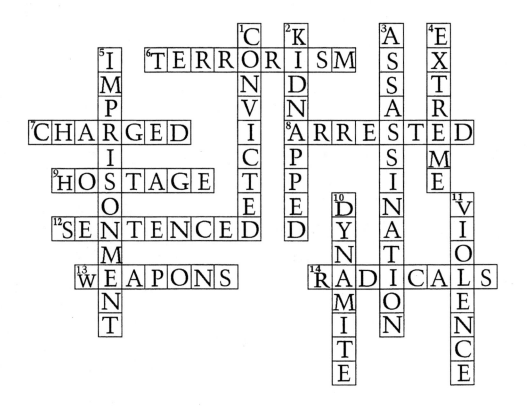

CREATE A CROSSWORD!

Puzzle B

Work with a partner to write clues for "Down." The other members of your group will write the clues for "Across." Your clues should be based on the content of Chapter 10 and should include a paragraph reference.

ASPECTS OF MY CULTURE

In Chapter 10, you read that most French Canadians want to preserve their language and culture. Culture is a very important part of every human being. We learn our culture from the adults around us when we are growing up: in our family, at school, from the media, from religion, from books, from art and music, and from everything that is part of our way of life.

Many people live in more than one culture. For example, many young people who came to Canada from other countries live within the culture of their parents at home and in their cultural community, but learn the culture of the larger Canadian society at school.

Culture has many aspects. Can you identify some aspects of your culture? Do you know where or how you learned the different aspects of your culture?

Prepare an oral presentation about your culture. You cannot read to the class, but you can look at notes that you have made. Use some of these headings to help organize your notes.

My culture consists of:
My language(s)
My religious beliefs
My role in the family
The food I like to eat or cook
The art I know about and value
The clothes I wear
The music I like
Great literature that I have read or heard
How I relate to the opposite sex
How I feel about the older people
How I feel about education
What I believe about work
How I relate to my neighbours
How I relate to my friends
How I relate to my classmates
How I relate to my teachers
How I relate to those in authority; police, government...

A suggestion:
Your classmates may be interested in seeing some family photos or artifacts representing aspects of your culture.

Chapter Title:

First major topic:

Second major topic:

Subtopic 1:

Subtopic 1:

Main points:

1.

2.

3.

4.

Subtopic 2:

Main points:

1.

2.

3.

4.

Subtopic 3:

Main points:

1.

2.

3.

Subtopic 2:

Chapter Title: CANADA'S ECONOMY AND CULTURE SINCE 1945

First major topic:
The Canadian Economy

Second major topic:
Canadian Culture

Subtopic 1:
Co-operation
between
Canada and
the U.S.

Subtopic 1:
What is Canadian culture?

Main points:

1. Canadian culture is
   different from American
   culture.

2. How American culture
   has influenced Canadian
   culture.

3. Canada's cultural
   industries.

4. Canadian culture and
   society.

Subtopic 2: Foreign
investment in Canada

Main points:

1. Canada's attitude
   toward American
   investments.

2. Advantages of
   American
   investment.

3. Disadvantages of
   American
   investment.

4. Government
   policies on foreign
   investment.

Subtopic 3:
Free trade

Main points:

1. Free trade has been
   a major issue in
   elections.

2. How Canada got a
   Free Trade Agree-
   ment with the
   United States.

3. Effects of the Free
   Trade Agreement
   in Canada

Subtopic 2: Case study

West Indians in Canada

A DELICATE BALANCE

The Partnership between Canada and the United States

Canadians often argue about the advantages and disadvantages of American investment in Canada. Various Canadian governments have questioned whether it is wise to increase our ties to the United States. Weigh the advantages and disadvantages of American investment in Canada yourself.

Review paragraphs 4-17 of Chapter 11.
Find the factors that you must weigh in making a decision about whether American investment is good or bad: these are aspects of Canadian life that would be affected by an increase or decrease in American investment. Record the factors in the appropriate column. The first one has been recorded for you.

Is it a good idea to increase American investment in Canada?

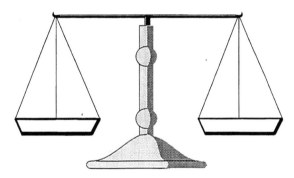

¶¶5, 6, 12: Advantages
Higher employment

¶¶7-12: Disadvantages
Canada exports raw materials to the U.S. and imports expensive manufactured products from the U.S.

I RECOMMEND...

Consider the effects on each area of Canadian life if U.S. investment increased. Advise the Canadian government of the policy it should pursue.

If you believe that the advantages outweigh the disadvantages, you will advise the Canadian government to increase U.S. investment. If you believe that the disadvantages outweigh the advantages, you will advise the Canadian government to decrease U.S. investment in Canada.

Write a letter to your Member of Parliament presenting your opinion on trade with the United States. Your letter should contain this information:

Your address

Date

Name of MP
House of Commons
Ottawa, Ont.
K1A 0A6

Dear _____,

I am one of your constitutents in ... I am writing to let you know my opinion on trade with the United States.

I believe that we should ... There are several reasons for my opinion.

First of all ... For example, ...

Also, ...

Finally ...

If we do not ... with the U.S., ... therefore, I ... suggest (advise, recommend that you, encourage, urge you to)

Yours sincerely,

Your name

FREE TRADE — A CENTURY OF CONTROVERSY: 1891-1988

The issue of free trade between Canada and the United States has caused contro-
versy in Canada for nearly a century. *Read ¶¶18-31 and complete the chart.*

Prime Minister?	Free trade?	Conflicts?	Details and reasons?	Results?
1891 Wilfrid Laurier	☐ Yes ☑ No	☑ Yes ☐ No	Laurier thought a free trade agreement would increase trade, but most Canadians disagreed because they thought that trade with Britain was more important.	Laurier lost the election.
1911	☐ Yes ☐ No	☐ Yes ☐ No		
1960	☐ Yes ☐ No	☐ Yes ☐ No		

Prime Minister?	Free trade?	Conflicts?	Details and reasons?	Results?
1970s	☐ Yes ☐ No	☐ Yes ☐ No		
1970s	☐ Yes ☐ No	☐ Yes ☐ No		
1980s	☐ Yes ☐ No	☐ Yes ☐ No		

NOT A LEG TO STAND ON

Freeze Trade or Free Trade?

Look at the political cartoon on page 191 and answer these questions:

1. Which two Canadian political parties disagree over the question of free trade with the United States?

   _____

2. Who are the two party leaders shown in the cartoon?

   _____

3. Look at the arguments that follow. Beside each, note whether it is a statement **for** or **against** the Free Trade Agreement and **write** the name of the political party that would agree with the statement.

Statements for and against free trade	For or against?	Political party?
Canadian companies will become more efficient and productive to compete with the rest of the world.	_____	_____
Canada will lose control of energy, investment and cultural programs.	_____	_____
Laws that have helped Canadian workers in the past will change.	_____	_____
The U.S. government could still make Canadians pay tariffs as a penalty.	_____	_____
Canadians will pay lower prices for some products.	_____	_____
Canadian factories and products will be able to sell more.	_____	_____

4. Look at the shields that the two leaders are carrying.

   What does the leader of the Conservative Party have on his shield? _____

   What do you think this symbolizes? _____

   What does the leader of the Liberal Party have on his shield? _____

   What do you think this symbolizes? _____

5. Look carefully at the horse that the Liberal party leader is riding.

   What do you notice about it?

   _____

   _____

   Why do you think the cartoonist drew the horse this way?

   _____

   _____

   What is the meaning of the idiom "not a leg to stand on"?

   _____

   _____

6. Do you think the cartoonist agrees with the Liberal Party or the Conservative Party? Why?

   _____

   _____

   _____

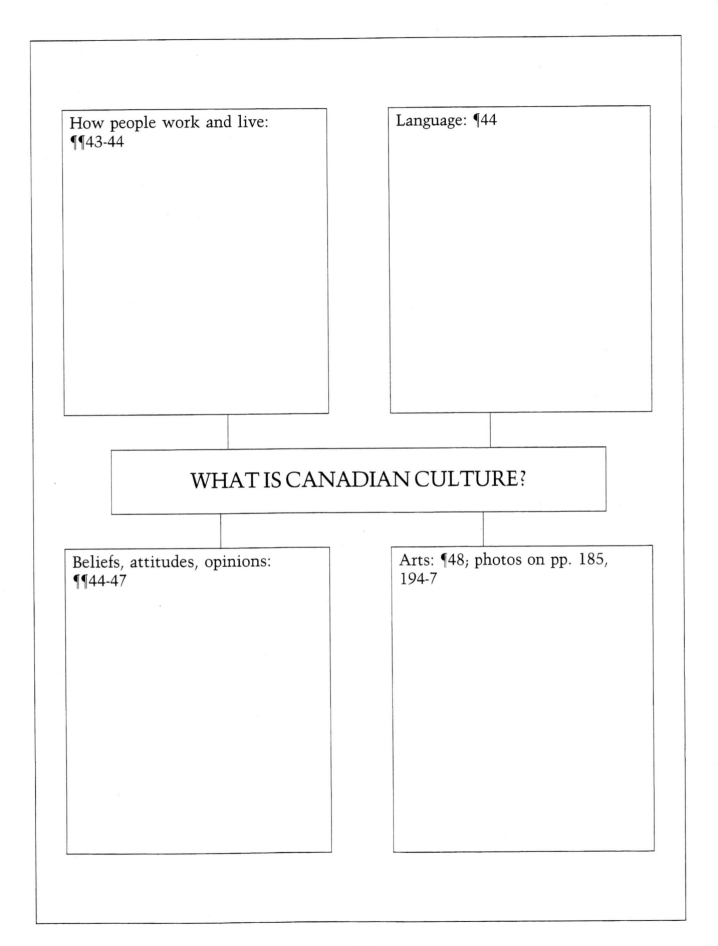

How people work and live: ¶¶43-44

Language: ¶44

WHAT IS CANADIAN CULTURE?

Beliefs, attitudes, opinions: ¶¶44-47

Arts: ¶48; photos on pp. 185, 194-7

WHY AND HOW CANADA PROMOTES CANADIAN CULTURE

Like people in many other parts of the world, Canadians want to protect and promote their culture. Why? How does the Canadian government do this?

Read ¶¶33-41 and match the reasons below with the correct Canadian institution. The first one is done for you.

Why?	*How*
Canadians need to know about their world.	CRTC
Canadians are worried that Canadians watch too much U.S. television.	CBC
Canadians are worried that Canadians watch too many U.S. films.	CRTC
Canadian writers, artists, musicians, dancers and filmmakers need more opportunities to express their culture.	NFB
Canadians need to protect or create jobs in the cultural industries.	Canada Council
The Canadian government needs more tax money!	CRTC

WHO INFLUENCES US?

Conducting and Reporting the Results of a Survey

Many Canadians are worried that American culture has too strong an influence on Canadian culture and Canadians. Conduct a survey to find out if this is true.

1. *Write a set of questions that you can use with each person you interview.* You need to find out:

The most recent movie your interviewee saw.

What _____ ?

Where the movie was made.

Where _____ ?

Your interviewee's favourite TV show.

What _____ ?

Where the TV show was made.

Where _____ ?

Your interviewee's favourite band or song.

What _____ ?

Where the song or band comes from.

Where _____ ?

Your interviewee's favourite sports team.

What _____ ?

Where the sports team comes from.

Where _____ ?

2. Interview 10 people and record their responses to your questions.

	Movie	Country	TV show	Country	Song or band	Country	Sports team	Country
1.								
2.								
3.								
4.								
5.								
6.								
7.								
8.								
9.								
10.								

3. *Calculate percentages.*

   Calculate the percentage of your total sample that watched ...

   A Canadian movie ____   An American   A movie from another
                            movie _____   country _____

   Calculate the percentage of your sample whose favourite TV show is ...

   Canadian _____   American _____   From another country
                                                     _____

   Calculate the percentage of your sample whose favourite music is ...

   Canadian _____   American _____   From another country
                                                     _____

   Calculate the percentage of your sample whose favourite sports team is...

   Canadian _____   American _____   From another country
                                                     _____

4. *State your findings.*
   Combine your figures with those of other students in your group and write statements about your combined results.

   We interviewed _____ students about their preferences in sports and entertainment. Here are our results:

   We found that _____ per cent of our sample watched an American movie recently; _____ per cent watched a Canadian movie and _____ per cent watched a movie from another country. Also, we found that _____ per cent of our sample _____, _____ per cent

   _____ ,

   and _____ per cent _____. Another

   finding was that _____

   _____

   _____. Finally, our

   results show that _____

   _____

   _____

5. *Draw conclusions.*

Are Canadians more influenced by American cultural products than Canadian cultural products?

I think _____

_____ because _____

_____

Is it important for the Canadian government to protect and promote Canadian culture?

In my opinion, the government _____

_____ because

_____

_____

CANADA'S ECONOMY AND CULTURE

Here are the word families of some of the words you read in Chapter 11.

Common nouns	Abstract nouns	Verbs	Adjectives
	agreement, disagreement	agree, disagree	agreeable, disagreeable
benefactor	benefit	benefit	beneficial
complaint (a legal term)	complaint	complain	complaining
creator	creation	create	creative
developer	development	develop	developed
economist	economy, economics	economize	economical
	expression	express	expressive
industrialist	industry	industrialize	industrial, industrialized
investor	investment	invest	invested
	influence	influence	influential
negotiator	negotiation	negotiate	negotiated
opponent	opposition	oppose	opposite, opposed
politician	policy	politicize, politick	political
	security, insecurity	secure	secure, insecure
supporter	support	support	supportive
technologist	technology		technological

Choose words from the word families to complete these sentences:

Canada's first Prime Minister, John A. Macdonald, encouraged American _____ in Canada as a way of helping Canada's _____ to expand.

Prime Minister Wilfrid Laurier was also a strong _____ of free trade. He believed that free trade with the United States would be _____ to Canadians. Many Canadians were _____ to free trade, and Laurier lost two elections over this issue.

Many Canadians feel that American _____ in Canada may _____ more problems than _____ for Canada. Prime Minister Pierre Trudeau tried to control the effects of American _____ on Canada's _____ and culture.

In his election campaign, Prime Minister Brian Mulroney told Canadians that free trade with the United States would lead to the _____ of more jobs. Most Canadians _____ free trade, but many businesspeople in Canada _____ the idea. The Free Trade Agreement became law after Brian Mulroney and the Conservatives won the election in 1988.

President Ronald Reagan of the United States _____ free trade with Canada because his government believed it would help American businesses sell more _____, agricultural, _____ and financial _____ and services in Canada.

Many Canadians involved in the arts believe that American cultural _____, such as book and magazine publishing, television, movies and music, are so _____ in Canada that Canadians are in danger of losing their own culture and identity.

Institutions such as the Canada Council and the CBC _____ Canadians to _____ their cultural and artistic indentity.

APPLYING FOR CANADIAN CITIZENSHIP

Take turns with a partner. One of you is applying to become a Canadian citizen; the other is an officer of the Court of Citizenship. The officer interviews the applicant and complete the following sections of the Application for Citizenship.

Section A   General   **Protected** (When completed)

1. Have you applied for Canadian citizenship before?
   No ☐   Yes ☐ If yes, give details.

2. In which official language do you wish to: English   French
   a) have your hearing with the citizenship judge?   ☐   ☐
   b) take the oath of citizenship?   ☐   ☐
   c) have your citizenship certificate prepared?   ☐   ☐

Section B   Personal Data

3. Marital status: Single ☐   Married ☐   Divorced ☐   Separated ☐   Widowed ☐

4. Mr. ☐   Mrs. ☐   Miss ☐   Ms. ☐
   Family name   Given name(s)

a)

b)

5. Home address   Mailing address (if different than home address)

Postal code   Postal code

Telephone   Area code   Area code
   Home ___ ___ - ___   Work ___ ___ - ___

6. Birth date   Place and country of birth   Present Nationality
   Y   M   D   Sex   Height   Colour of eyes
                                                      M ☐ F ☐   cm

7. Give details of any name change or aliases (see instructions).
   a) Your name at birth.

   b) Other names that you have used or now use, but will not be shown on the certificate, (e.g. nickname).

Section C   Immigration Data

8. Your name EXACTLY as it appears on your Canadian immigration document.
   Family name   Given name(s)

9. Date and place granted landed immigrant status IN CANADA.
   Y   M   D

10. Date and place of original entry to Canada, if different from date and place granted landed immigrant status.
    Y   M   D

11. Are you now or have you ever been under or included in an order of deportation from Canada?
    No ☐   Yes ☐ If yes, give details and provide any related documents.

Reprinted by permission of the Department of Citizenship and Immigration of Canada.

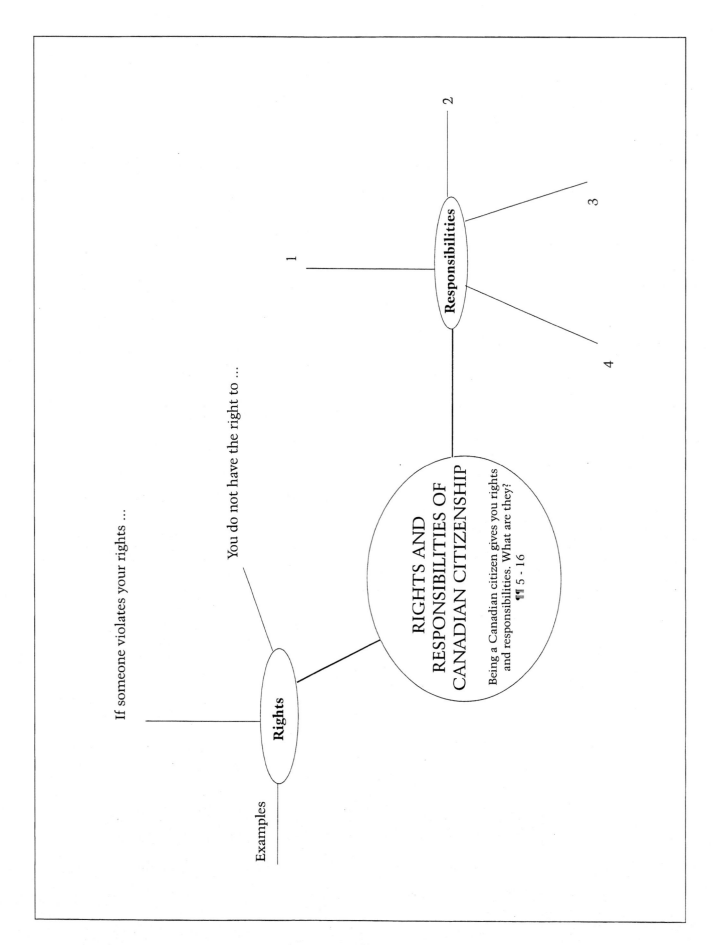

Examples

If someone violates your rights ...

You do not have the right to ...

Rights

RIGHTS AND RESPONSIBILITIES OF CANADIAN CITIZENSHIP

Being a Canadian citizen gives you rights and responsibilities. What are they?
¶¶ 5 - 16

Responsibilities

1

2

3

4

PROTECT YOUR RIGHTS!

Roleplay this case study about someone who experienced discrimination and present your roleplay to the class.

Tru Huynh is 40 years old. He has been working as a mechanic for a machinery company for many years. He is a qualified mechanic who does his job very well. His employer likes to have Tru on the job. Tru has decided to apply for a job closer to his home because he wants to go to his children's school to pick them up at the end of the day. His wife, Tien, also works very far away and cannot get to the school on time.

The company he applies to refuses to give him a job. The personnel officer who interviews him says that he is too old to work for them. Tru does not think this is fair. He discusses the problem with a friend, who advises him to take his case to the Human Rights Commission.

Tru writes to the Human Rights Commission. The officer who reads his letter thinks that they should investigate the case. The officer interviews Tru and then writes to the company where Tru applied for a job.

The personnel officer says that his company hires only mechanics who are younger than 25. The personnel officer explains that a good mechanic must have good eyesight and Tru wears glasses. The personnel officer insists that Tru is too old for the job and refuses to give him the job.

Assign these roles:

Tru
Tien
The personnel officer at the company
Tru's friend
A Human Rights Commission officer

Rehearse these scenes:

The discussion between Tru and his wife. Why is he going to apply for a new job?
The job interview with the personnel officer.
The discussion between Tru and his friend. What should he do?
The interview at the Human Rights Commission.

Present your roleplay to the class.

PROTECT YOUR RIGHTS!

Complete this cartoon story about someone who experienced discrimination. You can illustrate the dialogue on this page or you can create the whole cartoon on a large sheet of chart paper.

An employee in a department store is experiencing sexual harassment: a manager is making advances towards a younger worker of the opposite sex.

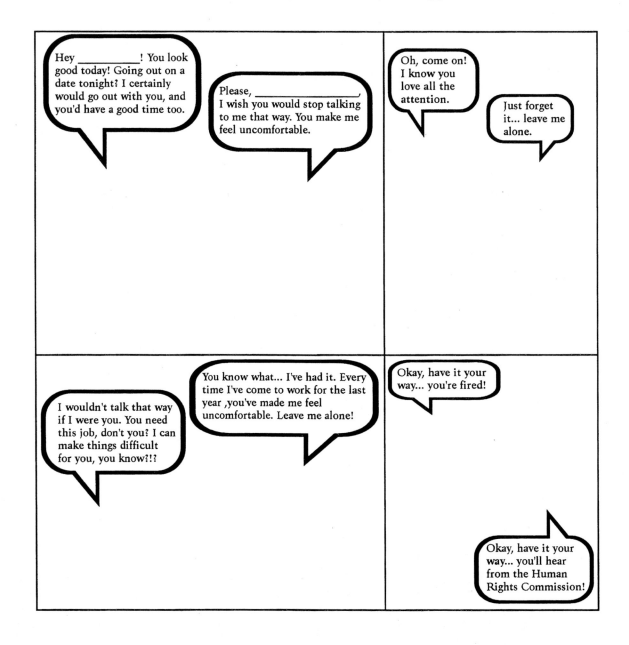

HOW TO FIND A GOVERNMENT SERVICE

The various responsibilities and powers of Canada's three levels of government are sometimes difficult to follow. The Blue Pages of your telephone book list the services provided by all three levels of government.

Share a telephone book with a partner and locate the Blue Pages. Find the page numbers for the following sections of the Blue Pages:

- Phone numbers and addresses for the government of Canada (the federal government).
- Phone numbers and addresses for your provincial government.
- Phone numbers and addresses for your city or municipal government.

Complete the chart by filling in five examples of the services provided by each of these three levels of government.

Federal Government Services	Provincial Government Services	Municipal Government Services

HOW TO USE THE BLUE PAGES

Identifying Key Terms

Sometimes, finding the correct telephone numbers and addresses for government services can be difficult. You might know what you need, but you don't know which word or phrase or **key term** *to look for in the Blue Pages.*

Below are the federal, provincial, and municipal responsibilities listed in your text on pages 207, 212 and 213.

In each cases, underline the word that you think is the key term you would look for in the Blue Pages.

Federal Responsibilities

- Unemployment insurance
- Collecting income tax and GST
- Controlling immigration Royal Canadian Mounted Police
- Operating prisons
- Canada Pension and Old Age Security payments
- Providing veterans' allowances and disability pensions
- Postal services
- Regulation of food and drugs
- Shipping and air travel

Provincial Responsibilities

- Providing education
- Providing health care
- Providing police services
- Collecting provincial taxes
- Building, maintaining and repairing highways
- Licensing of drivers and motor vehicles
- Promoting tourism
- Municipal governments
- Providing workers' compensation
- Environmental protection

Municipal Responsibilities

- Collecting property taxes
- Snow and garbage removal
- Animal control
- Licensing new businesses
- Controlling the heights of property fences
- Putting up stop lights
- Building sewers and roads
- Noise control
- Providing city police services
- Safety inspections of new and renovated buildings
- Fire protection

In the Government of Canada section of the Blue Pages, locate the address and telephone number for the Court of Citizenship in your area.

Phone the Court of Citizenship. You will probably be connected to an automatic answering system. Listen to the messages and get this information:

Office hours _____

The documents you need to bring with you to apply for Canadian citizenship.

_____

The application fee _____

WHAT SERVICES DO GOVERNMENTS PROVIDE?

Complete this chart comparing Canadian government services with services that other countries provide. Start by listing the countries that your group members come from. Then ask questions to get the information you need to complete the chart. Mark your chart with ✓ for "Yes" and X for "No."

	Canada				
Health care					
Education					
Welfare					
U.I.					
Police					
Housing					
Water					
Utilities					
Phone service					
Mail service					
Transportation					
Other					

Does Canada provide more or fewer services than most of the other countries?

Canada _____ than most other countries.

How do Canadians pay for these services?

Canadians _____

Do you think the government should provide these services? Why or why not?

I think _____

because _____

_____

WHO'S WHO IN CANADIAN GOVERNMENT?

Read ¶¶22-37 and complete the chart.

	How do you get this position?	What do you have to do in this position?
Queen ¶¶24-25		
Governor General ¶¶26-28		
Prime Minister ¶¶29		
Cabinet ministers ¶¶30-31		
Senators ¶¶32-33		
Members of Parliament ¶¶34-35		
Supreme Court judges ¶¶36		
Civil servants ¶37		

ELECTIONS IN CANADA

Use words from this list, or different forms of these words, to complete the paragraphs that follow:

candidate	citizen	enumerate	register	polling
riding	involved	booth	office	campaign
election	ballot	private	participate	eligible

Who is _____ to vote in federal _____ in Canada?
You can vote if you are a Canadian _____, you live in the _____, you are over 18, and you are _____ on the voter's list.

How do you get on the voters' list?
_____ come to your house and ask questions about who lives there. If you receive a notice of _____ and your name is not there, even though you are _____ to vote, you should call the number on the notice.

How do you vote?
On _____ day you go to the _____ station. The vote in Canada is _____; no one has the right to know which _____ you choose. You receive a _____ with the names of all the _____ on it. Then you go inside a voting _____ and mark your choice with an "X."

How can I _____ in an election?
You can have a sign in your front yard or window to show that you support a particular _____. You can work for his or her _____ by giving out information and talking to your neighours. You can work as an _____. And you can even run for _____ yourself!

BECOMING A CANADIAN CITIZEN

People who were not born in Canada can apply to become Canadian citizens. Citizenship applicants have a hearing in the Citizenship Court, where the citizenship judge asks questions to make sure the applicant knows enough about Canada to be a good citizen.

Write 10 questions that you think a citizenship judge might ask. Then interview your partner and decide if he or she is ready to be a citizen.

1. _____
   _____

2. _____
   _____

3. _____
   _____

4. _____
   _____

5. _____
   _____

6. _____
   _____

7. _____
   _____

8. _____
   _____

9. _____
   _____

10. _____
    _____

ANSWER KEY

Jigsaw Word Puzzle: Chapter 1

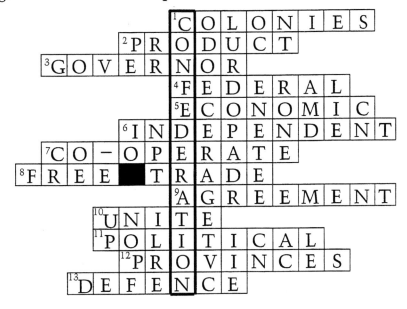

The hidden word is "Confederation." It means "joining together."

ANSWER KEY

Expansion of the Country: Chapter 3

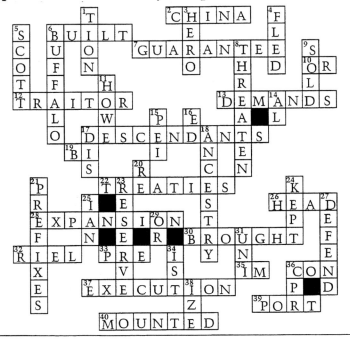

ANSWER KEY

All About Economics: Chapter 7

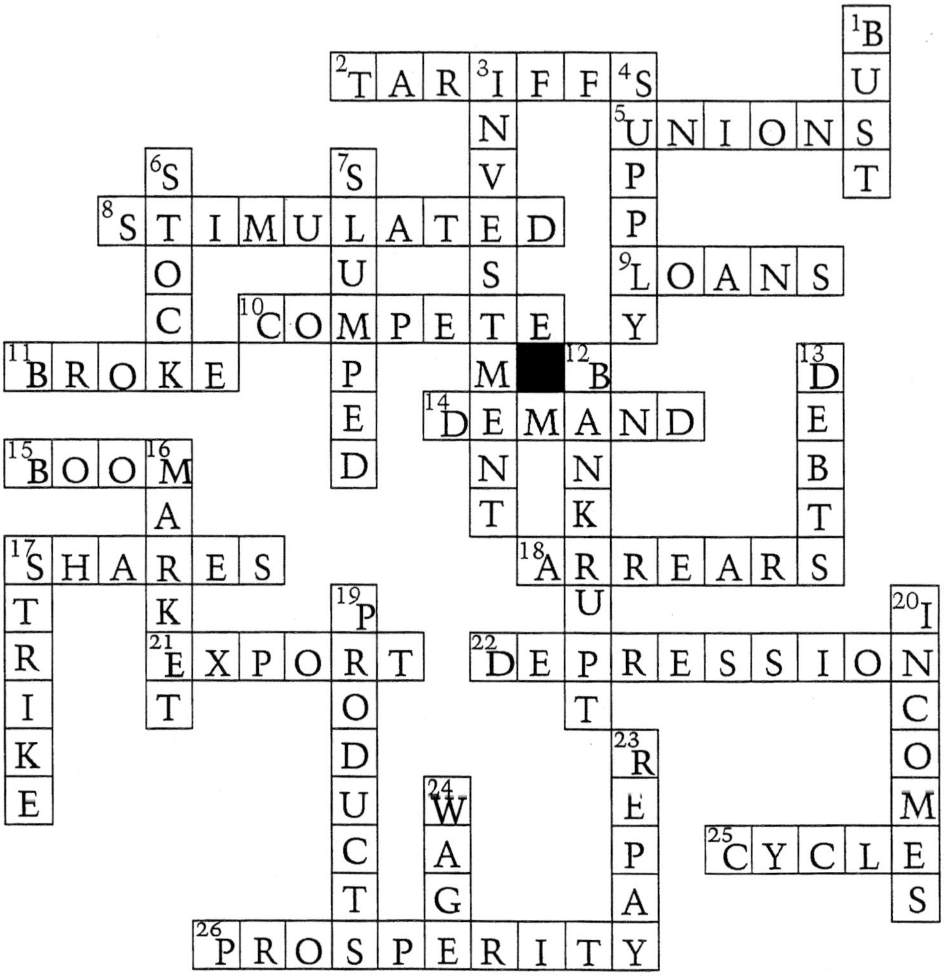
1 BUST
2 TARIFFS
3 INVESTMENT
4 SUPPLY
5 UNIONS
6 STOCK
7 SLUMPED
8 STIMULATED
9 LOANS
10 COMPETE
11 BROKE
12 BANKRUPT
13 DEBTS
14 DEMAND
15 BOOM
16 MARKET
17 SHARES
STRIKE
18 ARREARS
19 PRODUCT
20 INCOMES
21 EXPORT
22 DEPRESSION
23 REPAY
24 WAGE
25 CYCLE
26 PROSPERITY